50 Activities for Teaching Emotional Intelligence

The Best From Innerchoice Publishing

Level III: High School

Introduction and Theory
by
Dianne Schilling

Innerchoice Publishing, Torrance, California

Cover Design: Doug Armstrong Graphic Design

Illustrations: Roger Johnson, Zoe Wentz, and Dianne Schilling

INNERCHOICE PUBLISHING
P.O. BOX 1185
TORRANCE, CA 90505
Tel. (310) 816-3085 Fax (310) 816-3092

Contents

Over the last decade or so "wars" have been proclaimed, in turn, on teen pregnancy dropping out, drugs, and most recently violence. The trouble with such campaigns, though, is that they come too late, after the targeted problem has reached epidemic proportions and taken firm root in the lives of the young. They are crisis intervention, the equivalent of solving a problem by sending an ambulance to the rescue rather than giving an inoculation that would ward off the disease in the first place. Instead of more such "wars," what we need is to follow the logic of prevention, offering our children the skills for facing life that will increase their chances of avoiding any and all of these fates.

—Daniel Goleman

How to Use . . .
50 Activities for Teaching Emotional Intelligence

Inspiration and Origins

This activity guide is a collection of the most popular and effective emotional literacy activities offered by Innerchoice Publishing over the past ten years. The activities have been compiled expressly for the purpose of helping you apply the theory and recommendations of authorities in the field of brain-based education and emotional learning, including behavioral scientist and best-selling author Daniel Goleman (*Emotional Intelligence: Why It Can Matter More Than IQ*).

Like many educators, Goleman views "the curriculum" as a plan for ongoing comprehensive age-appropriate lessons taught school wide. Based on this definition, he is correct in concluding that very few schools currently have an emotional intelligence curriculum. Goleman asserts, "In theory, there is no reason why such a curriculum could not be taught in every school nationwide. It already exists in many, but only in bits and pieces...not as a fully developed, step-by-step curriculum."

Over the years, Innerchoice Publishing has contributed hundreds of "bits," "pieces" and fully-developed programs to thousands of schools throughout the country. You are invited to use this newest contribution to the EQ curricular mosaic as:

- the core of your emotional literacy curriculum

- a specialized EQ supplement to your existing curriculum

The bottom line is, don't neglect or take for granted the emotional life of your students. Feelings, self-awareness, life skills, conflict management, self-esteem, and all of the other developmental areas now identified as affecting emotional intelligence are critically important. An impressive array of brain-based research supports the validity of time and energy spent by educators in these domains. Emotions are not unruly remnants of stone-age survival to be hushed and otherwise ignored while we develop cognitive skills. Emotions drive our behavior, shape our values, and predispose us to choose one course of action over others. Emotional and rational skills are equally important interdependent components of human intelligence.

Unit Organization

The ten units in this guide each contain five activities, and comprise a complete emotional literacy curriculum. They are:

• *Self-awareness*

Knowing the likes, dislikes, hopes, preferences, cultural heritage, talents, shortcomings, and other uniquenesses that make up the individual. Becoming aware of inner and outer states and processes.

• *Managing Feelings*

Building a vocabulary for feelings; knowing the relationship between thoughts, feelings and actions; accurately reading feeling cues in others and responding appropriately; realizing what is behind feelings (e.g. the primary feelings underlying anger) and learning how to constructively express and control feelings.

• **Decision Making**

Examining what goes into making decisions; learning a step-by-step process for decision making; applying the process to real issues.

• **Managing Stress**

Understanding what stress is, where it comes from, and how it affects daily living; learning to use exercise, diet, guided imagery, relaxation methods, and attitude changes to control and relieve stress.

• **Personal Responsibility**

Examining actions and knowing their consequences; learning when and how to say no; recognizing the existence of personal choice in almost all situations; taking responsibility for decisions and actions.

• **Self-concept**

Establishing a firm sense of identity and feeling esteem and acceptance of oneself; monitoring "self-talk" to catch negative messages such as internal put-downs; acknowledging the talents and abilities of self and others.

• **Empathy**

Taking the perspective and understanding the feelings of others; developing caring and compassionate attitudes.

• **Communications**

Learning and practicing effective communication skills; using I-statements instead of blame; listening actively.

• **Group Dynamics**

Working self-reflectively in groups while monitoring behaviors and roles; practicing cooperation and interdependence; knowing when and how to lead and when to follow.

• **Conflict Resolution**

Understanding that conflict is normal and potentially productive; learning how to fight fair with others; learning and practicing a variety of conflict-resolution strategies, including win-win approaches to negotiating, compromise, and problem-solving.

Each of the ten units contains three group activities and two fully developed Circle Sessions, along with a list of additional Circle Session topics, which allow you to repeat the impact of the powerful circle process for many weeks. Before you lead your first Circle Session, be sure to read the section, "EQ Super Strategy: The Circle Session" beginning on page 19.

Many of the activities include handouts, called "Experience Sheets," for you to duplicate and distribute to students. Experience sheets are written in a conversational style and speak directly to the individual student. Directions for their use are imbedded in the printed procedure for leading each activity.

The units are arranged in a suggested order, but may be implemented with considerable flexibility. We encourage you to maintain an agile, expansive attitude as you move through (or skip among) the units. Allow the reactions of students to spark new ideas for strengthening emotional literacy skills in each topic area.

Finally, please make any adjustments necessary to accommodate the interests, abilities, cultural backgrounds and learning styles of your students. Your experience and regular contact with students put you in an ideal position to interpret signals regarding relevancy and modify the activities accordingly.

Schooling the Emotional Mind

Young people have two minds — one that thinks and one that feels. An inch or so beneath the curls, buzz jobs and baseball caps, just behind the contact lenses and lashes, sit two systems operating two different yet interdependent intelligences: rational (IQ) and emotional (EQ). How young people function each day and throughout life is determined by both. Rational intelligence cannot perform well without emotional intelligence, and emotional intelligence benefits from the cool cognitive judgments of the rational mind. When the two perform together smoothly and efficiently, emotional intelligence rises and so does intellectual ability.

Thanks to psychologist and author Daniel Goleman, the term *Emotional Intelligence* has become part of our daily lexicon. Goleman's best-seller *Emotional Intelligence: Why It Can Matter More Than IQ* , a superb presentation of research from education, medicine, and the behavioral and brain sciences, forms the basis for much of the ensuing discussion as well as the accompanying strategies and activities.

What Is Emotional Intelligence?

The American Heritage Dictionary defines emotion as "an intense mental state that arises subjectively rather than through conscious effort and is often accompanied by physiological changes" and as "the part of the consciousness that involves feeling; sensibility."

The word *emotion* is a derivative of the Latin root, *movere*, to move. Anyone who has experienced intense joy, desire, anger, or grief knows that emotions are anything but static mental states. Emotions are something we *do*.

Emotions shift our attention and propel us into action, rapidly organizing the responses of different biological systems — facial expression, muscle tone, voice, nerves, hormones — and putting us in optimum condition to respond. Emotions serve to establish our position relative to our environment, pulling us toward certain people, objects, actions, and ideas, and pushing us away from others. They allow us to defend ourselves in dangerous situations, fall in love, protect the things we value, mourn significant loss, and overcome difficult obstacles in the pursuit of goals.

The words *emotion* and *motivation* are closely related. In order to be strongly motivated we have to *feel* strongly. We are moved to *do* things, and we are moved *by* things. In Goleman's words, "Every strong emotion has at its root an impulse to action; managing those impulses is basic to emotional intelligence."

The terms *emotional intelligence, emotional literacy, emotional competence,* and *emotional competencies* are used in varying contexts throughout these pages. *Emotional intelligence* is the capacity to acquire and apply information of an emotional nature, to feel and to respond emotionally. This capacity resides in the emotional brain/mind. *Emotional literacy* and *emotional competence* are used interchangeably to describe the relative ability to experience and productively manage emotions. The shorthand for these terms is EQ. *Emotional competencies* are skills and attributes — self-awareness, empathy, impulse control, listening, decision making, anger management — whose level of development determines the strength of our emotional intelligence and the degree of our emotional competence.

The Sentry and the Strategist

Experts and explorers in the field of brain-based education have known or suspected for many years that emotions are the ignition switch and the octane for learning. Curriculum developers in the self-esteem arena (including this publisher) have been developing emotional intelligence under the guise of self-esteem and life-skills education for at least two decades. However, not until Goleman's book have we seen such a startling configuration of scientific evidence — case after case demonstrating the power of the emotional mind to override rational intelligence for both good and bad consequences.

The Sentry

A small structure in the limbic region of the brain, the *amygdala*, is the center of the emotional mind. All incoming data to the brain pass through the amygdala where they are instantly analyzed for their emotional value before going to the cerebral cortex for processing. Data leaving the amygdala carry an emotional charge, which, if sufficiently powerful, can override reasoned thinking and logic.

The amygdala is the specialist in emotional matters, the storehouse of emotional memory, and the seat of passion. The amygdala allows us to recognize the *personal significance* of daily events, which in turn provoke pleasure, stir compassion, arouse excitement, and incite rage.

The amygdala plays the role of sentry, scanning every incident for signs of trouble. Far quicker than the rational mind, it charges into action without regard for the consequences.

In an emotional emergency, the amygdala proclaims a crisis, recruiting the rest of the brain to its urgent agenda. Goleman calls this an *emotional hijacking*, because it occurs instantaneously, moments before the thinking brain has had a chance to grasp what is occurring and decide on the best coarse of action.

Emptying the mailbox at the end of her driveway, Marci senses a blur of movement across the street and looks up to see an elderly woman stumbling to the ground. A man is sprinting down the sidewalk with something dangling from his hand. Mail scattering in her wake, Marci flies across the street and after the man, screaming "Drop it," "Drop it." A purse bounces from the sidewalk to the gutter. Marci sees it but continues running, finally slowing to a jog as the snatcher disappears over a fence.

This is an example of an emotional hijacking. What Marci did wasn't rational. She neither witnessed a crime nor checked with the assumed victim; she didn't even see the purse until it hit the ground. Marci's emotional mind spliced together a few visual cues and produced a small feat of heroism which she had no opportunity to evaluate until it was over. What Marci felt as she jogged back to sooth her elderly neighbor, was an abating storm of outrage. Marci's own purse had been stolen a few months earlier.

In moments of crisis or intense passion, such as Marci's, the habits of the emotional brain dominate, for better or for worse. That is why, after an emotional hijacking, we express surprise at our own behavior. "I probably shouldn't have done that. I don't know what came over me," was Marci's rational evaluation moments after she returned the purse and reflected on her behavior.

The warp speed responses of the emotional mind take place without entering conscious awareness. Their purpose is to protect us from danger — to keep us alive. Our earliest ancestors needed these split-second reactions in situations where decisions had to be made instantly. Run or fight. Hide or attack. Actions that spring from the emotional mind have been measured at a few thousandths of a second and carry an overwhelming sense of certainty.

The Strategist

The critical networks on which emotion and feeling rely include not only the limbic system (amygdala), but also the neocortex — specifically the prefrontal lobes, just behind the forehead. This part of the emotional brain is able to *control* feelings in order to reappraise situations and deal with them more effectively. It functions like the control room for planning and organizing actions toward a goal. When an emotion triggers, within moments the prefrontal lobes analyze possible actions and choose the best alternative.

In the wake of intense fear or anger, for example, the neocortex is capable of producing a calmer, more appropriate response. It can even muffle emergency signals sent out by the amygdala. However, this mechanism is slower, involving more circuitry.

In Marci's case, control came too late. It isn't that she threw caution to the winds. Her own safety did not become a consideration until after the chase was over.

Internal Battles

So far, the amygdala and neocortex sound like perfect partners, the alert sentry signaling danger and the cool strategist selecting prudent courses of action. But the sentry can easily overreact, and powerful emotions can disrupt our ability to think and reason. Fear can render us mute or maniacal; anger can make us lash out visciously.

In such moments, the circuits from the amygdala to the prefrontal lobes are creating neural static, sabotaging the ability of the prefrontal lobe to maintain working memory. That's why we complain that we "can't think straight" when we are upset.

These emotional circuits, and the automatic reactions they convey, are sculpted by experience throughout childhood. Emotionally-driven automatic responses are usually learned very early — as early as four years of age. According to Goleman, all it takes is for some feature of the present situation to resemble a situation from the past. The instant that feature is recognized by the emotional mind, the feelings that went with the past event are triggered. *The emotional mind reacts to the present as if it were the past.* The reaction is fast and automatic, but not necessarily accurate or appropriate to the situation at hand. Frequently we don't even realize what is happening. Goleman describes it like this:

The emotional mind uses associative logic. It takes elements that symbolize reality or trigger a memory of it to be the same as reality. While the rational mind makes logical connections between causes and effects, the emotional mind connects things that have similar, striking features. The rational mind reasons with objective evidence; the emotional mind takes its beliefs to be absolutely true and discounts evidence to the contrary. That's why it's futile to try to reason with someone who is emotionally upset. Reasoning is out of place and carries no weight. Feelings are self-justifying.

The Impact of Emotional Intelligence

Emotions impact every area of life: health, learning, behavior, and relationships.

Young people who are emotionally competent— who manage their own feelings well, and who recognize and respond effectively to the feelings of others — are at an advantage in every area of life, whether family and peer relationships, school, sports, or community and organizational pursuits. Young people with well-developed emotional skills are also more likely to lead happy and productive lives, and to master the habits of mind that will assure them personal and career success as adults.

In homes and schools where emotional intelligence is nurtured with the same concern as IQ, young people tolerate frustration better, get into fewer fights, and engage in less self-destructive behavior. They are healthier, less lonely, less impulsive, and more focused. Human relationships improve, and so does academic achievement.

Health

There is no longer any question that emotions can profoundly affect health. Science used to believe that the brain and nervous system were separate and distinct from the immune system. In fact, the two systems are in close communication, sending messages back and forth continuously. Furthermore, chemical messengers which operate in both the brain and the immune system are concentrated *most heavily* in neural areas that regulate emotion. Here are just a few of the implications:

- Inhibiting or constraining emotions compromises immune function. People who hide their feelings or refuse to talk about significant emotional upsets are at higher risk for a variety of health problems.

- Anger, and other negative emotions are toxic to the body and pose dangers comparable to smoking cigarettes.

- Studies have linked the colds and upper respiratory infections to emotional upsets that occurred three to four days prior to the onset of symptoms.

- Numerous studies have shown that positive, supportive relationships are good medicine, bolstering immune function, speeding recovery time, and prolonging life. The prognosis for people in ill health who have caring family and friends is dramatically better than for people without emotional support.

Learning

Almost all students who do poorly in school lack one or more elements of emotional intelligence. Study after study has shown that competence in emotional skills results not only in higher academic achievement on the part of students, but in significantly more instructional time on the part of teachers. Emotionally competent young people are far less disruptive and require fewer disciplinary interventions.

Furthermore, academic intelligence, as measured by IQ and SAT scores, is not a reliable predictor of who will succeed in life. IQ contributes about 20 percent to factors that determine life success, which leaves 80 percent to other forces. Numerous studies have shown that IQ has minimal impact on how individuals lead their lives — how happy they are, and how successful. One major reason is that while cognitive skills are tied to IQ, desire and motivation are products of emotional intelligence. Young people who are emotionally competent have an increased desire to learn and to achieve, both within school and without. Positive emotions — excitement, curiosity, pride — are the fuel that drives motivation. Passion moves young people toward their goals.

Behavior

Violence and disorder in America's schools have reached crisis proportions. Teachers who once dealt with mischievous, unruly students and an occasional temper tantrum are now demanding emergency phones in their classrooms, security guards in the hallways, and metal detectors at the gates. As long as such conditions continue, all education suffers. Rates of teen suicide, pregnancy, and drug abuse testify to the need for emotional literacy: self-awareness, decision-making, self-confidence, and stress management.

Relationships

Young people who are effective in social interactions are capable of understanding their peers. They know how to interact with other teens and adults — flexibly, skillfully, and responsibly — without sacrificing their own needs and integrity. They have a good sense of timing and are effective at being heard and getting help when they need it. Socially competent young people can process the nonverbal as well as verbal messages of others, and recognize that the behaviors of one person can affect another. They take responsibility for their actions.

Young people who cannot interpret or express emotions feel frustrated. They don't understand what's going on around them. They are frequently viewed as strange, and cause others to feel uncomfortable. Without social competence, teens can easily misinterpret a look or statement and respond inappropriately, yet lack the ability to express their uncertainty or clarify the intentions and desires of others. They may lack empathy and be relatively unaware of how their behavior affects others.

Early Development

The first school for emotional literacy is the home. How parents treat their children has deep and lasting consequences for their emotional life.

In order to help children deal constructively with their emotions, parents must themselves have a reasonable degree of emotional literacy. The children of emotionally competent parents handle their own emotions better, are more adept at soothing themselves when they are upset, enjoy better physical health, are better liked by their peers, are more socially skilled, have fewer behavior problems, greater attention spans, and score higher on achievement tests.

Parents who ignore or show a lack of respect for their child's feelings, or who accept any emotional response as appropriate, are putting their child in peril not only for emotional development, but for intellectual development as well.

Bullies — children and young people who tend toward violence — have parents who ignore them most of the time, show little interest in their lives, yet punish them severely for real or perceived transgressions. These parents are not necessarily mean-spirited, they are usually repeating parenting styles that were practiced on them in childhood. Intellectually, they may want the best for their children, but have no inkling how to achieve it.

The emotional skill that violent children lack above all others is empathy. They are unable to feel what their victim is feeling, to view the situation through the eyes of the other child. In many cases, this lack of empathy is due to parental abuse. Abuse kills empathy.

Children who are repeatedly abused often suffer from post-traumatic stress disorder (PTSD). When a child's life is in danger and there is nothing the child can do to escape the peril, the brain actually changes.

A structure within the brain of children with PTSD secrets extra-large doses of brain chemicals in response to situations that are reminders of traumatic events, even when present events hold little or no threat. Oversecretions also occur from the pituitary gland, which alerts the body to danger and stimulates the fight or flight response. Thus, PTSD is a *limbic disorder*.

The good news is that the behavior of emotionally troubled children — bullies and children with PTSD — can change. The emotional circuitry can be rewired through relearning.

Emotional Windows

Research indicates that being bold or shy, upbeat or melancholy is at least partially genetic. Children may be predisposed to a certain temperament based on the relative excitability of the amygdala. However these innate emotional patterns can be improved with the right experiences.

Early emotional learning poses a similar problem. Synaptic connections are formed very quickly, in a matter of hours or days. In Goleman's words, "Experience, particularly in childhood, sculpts the brain."

The key skills of emotional intelligence each have a critical learning period extending over several years in childhood and adolescence. Massive sculpting of neural circuits takes place during these periods, each of which represents an optimal "emotional window" for learning specific skills. Once the emotional brain learns something, it never lets it go; once a window is closed, the pathway is forever etched. That's why changing in adulthood is so difficult. In fact, the patterns probably never change, though they can be controlled through new insights and with new learned responses.

The responses of the amygdala are well established long before a child leaves elementary school; however, the frontal lobes which regulate the limbic impulse mature into adolescence. Through skills and habits acquired at later ages, children can still learn to control their feelings, turn down the emotional thermostat, and substitute positive behaviors for negative.

Gender Differences

Girls receive significantly more education regarding emotions from their parents than do boys. In discussion, play, and fantasy, mothers cover a wider range of emotions with their daughters than with their sons.

Combine this greater knowledge with the fact that girls develop language skills more quickly than do boys and it is clear why girls find it easier to articulate their feelings and to use verbal exploration of feelings as substitutes for physical confrontations and fights, a difference that behavioral scientists have measured at about age 13. The chart summarizes gender differences in emotional intelligence.

Girls at 13:	Boys at 13:
• are adept at reading verbal and nonverbal emotional signals and expressing feelings.	• are adept at expressing anger
• experience a wide range of emotions with intensity and volatility.	• minimize emotions having to do with vulnerability, guilt, fear, and hurt.
• have learned to use tactics like ostracism, gossip, and indirect vendettas as substitutes for aggression.	• are confrontational when angry
• see themselves as part of a web of connectedness.	• take pride in a lone, tough-minded independence and autonomy

Controlling Emotions

If the sentry (the amygdala) and the neural pathways can't be changed, then the primary goal of emotional education is to improve the skills of the strategist — the neocortex. As we've seen, the neocortex is capable of managing the amygdala by reshaping its responses. Young people will still have their emotional outbursts, but can learn to control how long they last and the behaviors they produce.

Psychotherapy is a classic example of this process, with the client engaging in systematic emotional relearning. Therapy teaches people to control their emotional responses. Consistent positive discipline — the kind that focuses on feelings underlying behavior and on identifying alternatives to unacceptable behavior — accomplishes the same thing.

The ability to bring out-of-control emotions back into line results in what our parents and grandparents called *emotional maturity*. Present terminology labels it *emotional competence*, the "master aptitude."

Self-Awareness

The first step in getting young people to control their emotional responses is to help them develop self-awareness. Through self-awareness, young people learn to give ongoing attention to their internal states, to know what they are feeling when they are feeling it, to identify the events that precipitate upsets and emotional hijackings, and to bring their feelings back under control. Goleman defines self-awareness as:

...awareness of a feeling or mood and our thoughts about the feeling. ...a slight stepping-back from experience, a parallel stream of consciousness that is "meta": hovering above or beside the main flow, aware of what is happening rather than being immersed and lost in it.

Self-awareness allows young people to manage their feelings and to recover from bad moods more quickly. Teens who are self-aware don't hide things from themselves. Labeling feelings makes them their own. They can talk about fear, frustration, excitement, and envy and they can understand and speculate concerning such feelings in others, too.

Lacking self-awareness, young people may become engulfed by their feelings, lost in them, overwhelmed by them. Unawareness of what is going on in their inner and outer worlds sets the stage for lack of congruence between what they believe or feel and how they behave. Feelings of isolation ("I'm the only one who feels this way.") occur when young people are unaware that others experience the same range of feelings that they do. Without self-awareness young people never gain control over their lives. By default, their courses are plotted by others or by parts of themselves which they fail to recognize.

Self-awareness can take the form of nonjudgmental observation ("I'm feeling irritated.") or it can be accompanied by evaluative thoughts ("I shouldn't feel this way" or "Don't think about that.") Although in and of themselves, emotions are neither right nor wrong, good nor bad, these kinds of judgments are common and indicate that the neocortical circuits are monitoring the emotion. However, to try to abolish a feeling or attempt to take away a feeling in someone else only drives the emotion out of awareness, where its activity along neural pathways continues unmonitored and unabated — as neuroses, insomnia, ulcers, and communication failures of all kinds testify.

Managing Anger and Curbing Impulses

Eric started his day, not to the sounds of the birds or the local morning DJ, but to the jarring pre-dawn combat of his warring parents. The breakfast cereal was gone, the milk was sour, and there were no clean diapers for the baby whose fussing and screaming at length interrupted the din from the master bedroom. Accused of hurting the baby, Eric was scolded by his mother and slapped by his father. He fled the house without books or homework, almost missed the bus, and when he got to school was berated by his teacher for coming unprepared. At recess, Eric walked into the path of a speeding soccer ball, which stung his back and knocked him breathless. When he regained his wind, Eric found the boy who had kicked the ball and beat him until his face was bloody.

Eric had plenty of reasons to be angry. What he did not have, at least in this incident, were the internal skills or the external support system to help him process his feelings and prevent the anger from building.

Threats to life, security, and self-esteem trigger a two-part limbic surge: First, hormones called *catecholamines* are released, generating a rush of energy that lasts for minutes. Second, an adrenocortical arousal is created that can put a young person on edge and keep him there for hours, sometimes days. This explains why young people (including Eric) are more likely to erupt in anger over something relatively innocuous if the incident is preceded by an earlier upsetting experience. Though the two events may be completely unrelated, the anger generated by the second incident builds on the anger left over from the first. Irritation turns to anger, anger to rage, and rage erupts in violence.

Contrary to what many of us used to believe, when it comes to anger "letting it all out" is *not* helpful. Acting on anger will generally make a young person angrier, and each angry outburst will prolong and deepen the distress.

What does work is to teach young people to keep a lid on their feelings while they buy some time. If young people wait until they have cooled down, they can confront the other person calmly. When flooded with negative emotions the ability to hear, think, and speak are severely impaired. Taking a "time out" can be enormously constructive. However 5 minutes is not enough; research suggests that people need at least 20 minutes to recover from intense physiological arousal.

Research has also shown quite conclusively that it's possible for a young person to keep an angry mood going (and growing) just by thinking (and talking) about it.

> *Remembered or imagined experiences can create the same flood of chemistry as the experience itself*
> —Ellen Langer
> Harvard University, 1986

> *Thinking about a stressful situation produces the same bodily and mental responses as the experience itelf.*
> —American Medical Association
> Annual Research Conference, 1993

The longer a young person dwells on what made her angry, the more reasons and self-justifications she can find for being angry. So when encouraging young people to talk about their feelings, we need to be careful not to fan the flames.

Brooding fuels anger, but seeing things differently quells it. Reframing a situation is one of the most potent ways of controlling emotions.

Sadness: Shifting Gears

Depression and sadness are low-arousal states. When a young person is sad, it's as though a master gauge has turned down everything: mouth, eyes, head, shoulders, speech, energy, motivation, desire. Taking a jog is probably the last thing the young person feels like doing, but by forcing himself out the door and down the path, he will experience a lift.

The key seems to be shifting the mind from a low-arousal state to a high-arousal state. Exercise and positive distracting activities, like seeing a funny movie, turn up the master gauge, relieving sadness, melancholy, and mild depression. Another way to accomplish the shift is to engineer a small success, such as improving a skill, winning a game, or completing a project.

Humor is great at lifting teens out of the doldrums and can add significantly to their creativity and ability to solve problems, too. In studies documenting the effects of humor, people were able to think more broadly, associate more freely, and generate more creative solutions and decisions after hearing a joke.

The ability of humor to boost creativity and improve decision making stems from the fact that memory is "state specific." When we're in a good mood, we come up with more positive solutions and decisions. When we're in a bad mood, the alternatives we generate reflect our negativity.

Choosing to watch cartoons, shoot baskets, ride a bike, or spend a few minutes on the computer is a decision that takes place in the neocortex. The amygdala can't be stopped from generating sadness and melancholy, but young people can teach their neocortex a way out of the gloom.

Relationship Skills

If they are fortunate, youngsters are surrounded by people who give them attention, are actively involved in their lives, and model healthy, responsible interpersonal behavior. Core skills in the art of relationships are empathy, listening, mastery of nonverbal cues, and the ability to manage the emotions of others — to make accurate interpretations, respond appropriately, work cooperatively, and resolve conflicts.

Howard Gardner's theory of multiplicity intelligence includes two personal intelligences, *interpersonal* and *intrapersonal*. People with high interpersonal intelligence have the capacity to discern and respond appropriately to the moods, temperaments, motivations, and desires of others. Intrapersonal intelligence gives people ready access to their own feeling life, the ability to discriminate among their emotions, and accurate awareness of their strengths and weaknesses.

The personal intelligences equip young people to monitor their own expressions of emotion, attune to the ways others react, fine-tune their social performance to have the desired effect, express unspoken collective sentiments and guide groups toward goals. Personal intelligence is the basis of leadership.

Lacking personal intelligence, young people are apt to make poor choices related to such important decisions as who to befriend, emulate, date, and marry, what skills to develop and what career to pursue.

Components of Interpersonal Intelligence

- **Organizing groups:** directing, producing, leading activities and organizations

- **Negotiating solutions:** mediating, preventing and resolving conflicts, deal-making, arbitrating

- **Personal connections:** reading emotions and responding appropriately to the feelings and needs of others; teaming, cooperating

- **Social analysis:** insightful concerning the motives, concerns and feelings of others; able to size up situations

Components of Intrapersonal Intelligence

- **Self-knowledge and analysis:** having an accurate model of oneself and using that model to operate effectively in life; understanding own values, attitudes, habits, belief systems, strengths, weaknesses, and the motives that drive actions

- **Access to feelings:** the ability to discriminate among feelings and draw upon them to guide behavior; to identify and respond appropriately to own emotions

- **Personal organization:** the ability to clarify goals, plan, motivate, and follow through

- **Impulse control:** the ability to delay gratification; to deny impulse in the service of a goal

- **Fantasy and creativity:** the ability to nuture a rich and rewarding inner life

Empathy. All social skills are built on a base of emotional attunement, on the capacity for empathy. The ability to "walk in another's moccasins" is the foundation of caring and altruism. Violent people lack empathy.

Empathy is an outgrowth of self-awareness. The more we are able to understand our own emotions, the more skilled we are at understanding and responding to the emotions of others. Empathy plays heavily in making moral judgments. Sharing their pain, fear, or neglect is what moves us to help people in distress. Putting ourselves in the place of others motivates us to follow moral principles — to treat others the way we want to be treated.

These abilities have little to do with rational intelligence. Studies have shown that students with high levels of empathy are among the most popular, well adjusted, and high performing students, yet their IQs are no higher than those of students who are less skilled at reading nonverbal cues.

Empathy begins to develop very early in life. When infants and children under two witness the upset of another child, they react as if the distress were their own. Seeing another child cry is likely to bring them to tears and send them to a parent's arms.

From about the age of two on, when children begin to grasp the concept of their own separateness, they typically seek to console a distressed child by giving toys, petting, or hugging. In late childhood, they are able to view distress as an outgrowth of a person's condition or station in life. At this stage of development, children are capable of empathizing with entire groups such as the poor, the homeless, and victims of war.

Empathy can be developed through various forms of perspective-taking. In conflict situations, young people can be asked to listen to each other's feelings and point of view, and then to feed back or summarize the opposing perspective. Imagining the feelings of characters in literature as well as figures from current events and history is also effective. Combining role playing with these strategies makes them even more powerful.

Nonverbal Communication Skills. The mode of communication used by the rational mind is words; the mode preferred by the emotional mind is nonverbal. We telegraph and receive excitement, happiness, sorrow, anger, and all the other emotions through facial expressions and body movements. When words contradict these nonverbal messages — "I'm fine," hissed through clenched teeth — nine times out of ten we can believe the nonverbal and discount the verbal.

Acting out various feelings teaches young people to be more aware of nonverbal behavior, as does identifying feelings from videos, photos, and illustrations.

Emotions are contagious and transferrable. When two teens interact, the more emotionally expressive of the pair readily transfers feelings to the more passive. Again, this transfer is accomplished *nonverbally.*

Young people with high levels of emotional intelligence are able to attune to other young people's (and adult's) moods and bring others under the sway of their own feelings, setting the emotional tone of an interaction.

Guided by cultural background, young people learn certain display rules concerning the expression of emotions, such as minimizing or exaggerating particular feelings, or substituting one feeling for another, as when a young person displays confidence while feeling confused. As educators in a multiethnic, multiracial society, we need to be sensitive to a variety of cultural display rules, and help students gain a similar awareness.

Listening. Through listening, young people learn empathy, gather information, develop cooperative relationships, and build trust. Skillful listening is required for engaging in conversations and discussions, negotiating agreements, resolving conflicts and many other emotional and cognitive competencies.

Few skills have greater and more lasting value than listening. Unfortunately, listening skills are generally learned by happenstance, not by direct effort. The vast majority of children, teens and adults are either unable or unwilling to listen attentively and at length to another person.

Research shows that poor listening impedes learning and destroys comprehension. However, when students are taught to listen effectively, both comprehension and academic performance go up, along with classroom cooperation and self-esteem. Listening facilitates both emotional learning and relearning — strengthening and refining the analytical and corrective functions of the neocortex.

Conflict Management. Schools are rife with opportunities for conflict. From the farthest reaches of the playground to the most remote corners of the classroom, from student restrooms to the teacher's lounge, a thousand little things each day create discord. The causes are many.

Young people bring to school an accumulation of everything they've learned — all of their habits and all the beliefs they've developed about themselves, other people, and their world. Such diversity makes conflict inevitable. And because the conflict-resolution skills of most young people are poorly developed, the outcomes of conflict are frequently negative — at times even destructive.

Diversity also breeds conflict. Learning to understand, respect and appreciate similarities and differences is one key to resolving conflicts. Unfortunately most of us learn as children that there is only one right answer. From the moment this fallacious notion receives acceptance, the mind closes and vision narrows.

Prejudice cannot be eliminated, but the emotional learning underlying prejudice can be *relearned*. One way to accomplish relearning is to engineer projects and activities in which diverse groups work together to obtain common goals. Social cliques, particularly hostile ones, intensify negative stereotypes. But when young people work together as equals to attain a common goal — on committees, sports teams, performing groups — stereotypes break down.

Peer mediation programs offer another excellent avenue for relearning ineffective emotional responses to conflict. Mediators act as models, facilitators and coaches, helping their classmates develop listening, conflict resolution, and problem-solving skills.

Educating the Emotional Brain

Emotional intelligence is a core competence. To raise the level of social and emotional skills in students, schools need to focus on the emotional aspects of student's lives, which most currently ignore.

Unfortunately, in classes that stress subject-matter mastery, teaching is often devoid of emotional content. Too many educators believe that if somehow students master school subjects, they will be well prepared for life. Such a view suffers from a shallow and distorted understanding of how the human brain functions.

Joan Caulfield and Wayne Jennings, experts in brain-based education, specify four building blocks for incorporating emotional intelligence concepts in schools:

1. Safety, security, unconditional love and nurturing for every young person

2. Stimulating classroom environments which provide rich sensory input to the brain

3. Experiential learning; opportunities to engage skills, knowledge and attitudes in a wide variety of real life tests

4. Useful and timely performance feedback

Many of the competencies that should be addressed by educational programs in emotional literacy have been specified on the previous pages. A number of outlines are suggested by Goleman in his book, *Emotional Intelligence*. One of the most useful comes from Peter Salovey, a Yale psychologist whose list of emotional competencies includes five domains and incorporates Howard Gardner's theories on interpersonal and intrapersonal intelligences.

1. **Knowing one's emotions:** Self awareness — recognizing a feeling as it happens. Monitoring feelings from moment to moment

2. **Managing emotions:** Emotional competence. Handling feelings; ability to recover quickly from upsets and distress;

3. **Motivating oneself:** Marshaling emotions in order to reach goals; self-control and self-discipline; delaying gratification and stifling impulsiveness

4. **Recognizing emotions in others:** Empathy — the ability to recognize, identify, and feel what another is feeling.

5. **Handling relationships:** The ability to manage emotions in others; social competence; leadership skills

To be most effective, emotional literacy content and processes should be applied consistently across the curriculum and at all grade levels. Students should be afforded many opportunities for skill practice, through a combination of dedicated activities and the countless unplanned "teachable moments" that occur daily. When emotional lessons are repeated over and over, they are reflected in strengthened neural pathways in the brain. They become positive habits that surface in times of stress.

Weaving EQ Into the Curriculum

Teachers may resist the idea of adding new content areas to the curriculum. In most cases, demands on teacher time are already at or beyond the saturation point, but this needn't be an insurmountable obstacle to emotional education. Feelings are part of everything that children and adolescents do, and they can be part of everything they learn, too.

By incorporating lessons in emotional intelligence within traditional subject areas, we assist students to grasp the connections between realms of academic knowledge and life experience, and encourage them to utilize their multiple intelligences. This approach fits well with the concept of multidisciplinary teaching.

When a curriculum adheres to traditional straight and narrow subject areas and is devoid of emotional content, the subject matter is unlikely to "live" for students because of the curriculum's cold and reductionistic nature. With the world growing more complex by the minute, such an approach makes it extremely difficult for teens to integrate the parts and pieces of what they learn, much less apply them within a real-world context.

By suggesting relationships and posing the right questions, by being observant and noticing nonverbal signals, teachers can help to surface and deal with emotional elements in every lesson, no matter what the subject area. Likewise they can take moments of personal crisis and turn them into lessons in emotional competence.

The Facilitator Role

Some teachers gravitate toward lessons in emotional intelligence and need little encouragement; if you are one of those, great! However, if you are uncomfortable talking about feelings, consider enlisting the help of the school counselor. Very little in traditional teacher education prepared you for this role, so start slowly and concentrate on becoming an effective facilitator of emotional inquiry. Here are just a few suggestions:

1. Rethink (and help colleagues, administrators, and parents rethink) traditional approaches to discipline. Substitute skill development for punishment, using misbehavior, upsets, and fighting as opportunities to teach young people impulse control, conflict management, perspective taking, and awareness of feelings.

2. Strike a cooperative agreement with your school counselor. Invite the counselor to visit the classroom to lead emotional literacy activities.

3. Conduct class meetings to deal with issues and problems that the students submit for discussion. Create and decorate an "emotional mailbox" for the classroom, and encourage students to submit questions and problem descriptions.

4. Identify the dominant learning styles of individual students as a way of facilitating "flow." Flow is what we experience when we are so completely absorbed in a task or project that progress is effortless.

   In a state of flow, a student is completely relaxed yet intensely focused. Minimal mental energy is expended. Flow is characterized by an absence of limbic static and superfluous brain activity; emotions are positive and totally aligned with the task at hand.

An excellent way to encourage flow is to apply Gardner's theory of multiple intelligences, thus assuring that students engage in processes that are right for them and that utilize their competencies, learning styles, and talents. This allows the teacher to play to the strengths of students while attempting to shore up areas of weakness. As Goleman argues: "Pursuing flow through learning is a more humane, natural, and very likely more effective way to marshal emotions in the service of education."

5. Use cooperative learning principles and strategies. Cooperative learning optimizes the acquisition of subject-area knowledge while developing skills and concepts beyond those afforded by isolated study. Cooperation and collaboration mean that more information is discovered, processed, shared, and applied. And the fact that students process the information and find solutions along with their peers results in the development of a host of interpersonal and social skills.

By participating in team activities, students learn important lessons about group dynamics and develop extremely valuable communication skills. As students assimilate content, participating in team projects teaches them the value and skills of trust building, listening, respecting others' points of view, articulating ideas, planning, making choices, dividing the labor, encouraging others, taking responsibility, solving problems, compromising, managing and resolving conflicts, and celebrating team successes, to name just some of the benefits.

6. In addition to the emotional literacy activities in this book, be prepared for daily impromptu facilitation of emotional learning. For example:

- Work with students to bolster their sense of agency relative to the ups and downs in their lives. If a young person shows signs of depression, enlist the help of the school counselor. Teens who are candidates for depression seem to believe that bad things (for example, a low grade) happen to them because of some inherent flaw ("I'm stupid"), and that there is nothing they can do to change these conditions. More optimistic young people look for solutions, such as increased study time.

- Teach and counsel young people to control anger in these ways:

—Change the thoughts that trigger anger, reassessing the situation with a different (less provocative) point of view. Often this involves looking at the situation from the other person's perspective. "Perhaps Sue is having a bad day." "Maybe Juan doesn't feel well." Changing thoughts produces new feelings which displace the anger.

—Cool off through active exercise or distracting activities.

—Write down angry thoughts and then challenge and reappraise them.

—Identify and express the feelings that precede anger. Anger is often a secondary emotion, erupting in the wake of other feelings, like frustration, fear, or humiliation.

—Monitor the feelings and bodily sensations they experience when they're becoming angry. Learn to use these sensations as cues to stop and consider what is happening and what to do about it.

Organizational EQ

Let's take a minute to talk about ourselves — our own emotional intelligence, and the modeling we do for students. After all, educators have feelings, too.

Almost every organization, educational and otherwise, harbors a vast emotional undercurrent, a shadowy hidden world of unexpressed feeling. While on the surface we may appear calm and rational, underneath we are churning with emotions: resentment, jealousy, love, fear, guilt, revulsion, caring, pride, frustration, confusion, and joy.

We spend untold time and energy protecting ourselves from people we don't trust, avoiding problems we're afraid to broach, tiptoeing around performance issues, pretending to accept decisions with which we disagree, accepting jobs and assignments we don't want, and withholding our opinions and insights. What a waste. Emotions can help solve problems. Let's use them.

Emotional energy, whether positive or negative, moves us to action. Emotions are the source of passion, motivation, and commitment. When we share our feelings and opinions, work and work relationships are experienced as more vital and meaningful, and movement toward goals accelerates.

We must do everything we can to build schools where feelings are recognized, communication flows freely, and conflicts are handled productively. Where we can air complaints honestly, knowing that they will be viewed as helpful, where diversity is valued and nourished, and inclusion and interdependence are experienced at many levels.

The brightest futures belong to students who develop EQ along with IQ, and to school communities whose citizens have the courage to risk being human in the classroom, lunchroom, office, playground, workroom, and playing field.

When we *model* emotional intelligence, we employ the most potent teaching strategy of all.

EQ Super Strategy: The Circle Session

To achieve its goals, *50 Activities for Teaching Emotional Intelligence* incorporates a variety of proven instructional strategies. Activities include simulations, role plays, "experience sheets" for individual students to complete, and a host of small and large group experiments and discussions.

One of the most powerful and versatile of the instructional strategies used in this curriculum is the Circle Session. In each unit, two Circle Sessions are fully elaborated. These are followed by a list of additional Circle Session topics relevant to the unit topic. At first glance, the Circle Session — a small-group discussion process — is likely to appear deceptively simple. It is not. When used correctly, the Circle Session is unusually effective as a tool for developing self-awareness, the ability to understand and manage feelings, self-concept, personal responsibility, empathy, communication and group interaction skills.

The Circle Session is an ideal way to incorporate emotional learning in the classroom on a regular basis, and helps to form the four building blocks suggested by brain-based education experts Joan Caulfield and Wayne Jennings (see page 14). First, the Circle Session provides safety, security, unconditional love and nurturing to each young person. Second, Circle Session structure and procedures constitute a marked departure from traditional classroom teaching/learning approaches. Topics are stimulating in their ability to provoke self-inquiry. The ambiance is close yet respectful, over time causing intrapersonal defenses and interpersonal barriers to shrink and leading to new levels of group cohesiveness and creativity. Third, circle topics address real-life experiences and issues and the full range of emotions associated with them. And finally, the immediacy of the circle ensures that every young person's contributions are heard and accepted on the spot. The attentiveness of other circle members along with their verbal and nonverbal emotional and cognitive reactions constitute a legitimate and powerful form of affirming feedback.

Please take the time to read the following sections before leading your first circle. Once you are familiar with the process, implement Circle Sessions regularly and as frequently as you can.

An Overview of the Circle Session

Twenty-eight years of teaching the Circle Session process to educators world wide have demonstrated the power of the Circle Session in contributing to the development of emotional intelligence. To take full advantage of this process there are some things you need to know.

First, the topic elaboration provided under the heading, "Introduce the Topic," in each Circle Session is intended as a guide and does not have to be read verbatim. Once you have used Circle Sessions for a while and are feeling comfortable with the process, you will undoubtedly want to substitute your own words of introduction. We are merely providing you with ideas.

In your elaboration, try to use language and examples that are appropriate to the age, ability, and culture of your students. In our examples, we have attempted to be as general as possible; however, those examples may not be the most appropriate for your students.

Second, we strongly urge you to respect the integrity of the sharing and discussion phases of the circle. These two phases are procedurally and qualitatively different, yet of equal importance in promoting awareness, insight, and higher-level thinking in students. The longer you lead Circle Sessions, the more you will appreciate the instructional advantages of maintaining this unique relationship.

All Circle Session topics are intended to develop awareness and insight through voluntary sharing. The discussion questions allow students to understand what has been shared at deeper levels, to evaluate ideas that have been generated by the topic, and to apply specific concepts to other areas of learning.

In order for students to lead fulfilling, productive lives, to interact effectively with others, and to become adept at understanding and responding appropriately to the emotions of others, they first need to become aware of themselves and their own emotions. They need to know who they are, how they feel and function, and how they relate to others.

When used regularly, the *process* of the Circle Session coupled with its *content* (specific discussion topics) provides students with frequent opportunities to become more aware of their strengths, abilities, and positive qualities. In the Circle Session, students are listened to when they express their feelings and ideas, and they learn to listen to each other. The Circle Session format provides a framework in which genuine attention and acceptance can be given and received on a consistent basis.

By sharing their experiences and feelings in a safe environment, students are able to see basic commonalties among human beings — and individual differences, too. This understanding contributes to the development of self-respect. On a foundation of self-respect, students grow to understand and respect others.

As an instructional tool, the purpose of the Circle Session is to promote growth and development in students of all ages. Targeted growth areas include communication, self-awareness, personal mastery, and interpersonal skills. As students follow the rules and relate to each other verbally during the Circle Session,

they are practicing oral communication and learning to listen. Through insights developed in the course of pondering and discussing the various topics, students are offered the opportunity to grow in awareness and to feel more masterful — more in control of their feelings, thoughts, and behaviors. Through the positive experience of give and take, they learn more about effective modes of social interaction.

The Value of Listening

Many of us do not realize that merely listening to students talk can be immensely facilitating to their personal development. We do not need to diagnose, probe, or problem solve to help students focus attention on their own needs and use the information and insights in their own minds to arrive at their own conclusions. Because being listened to gives students confidence in their ability to positively affect their own lives, listening is certainly the facilitative method with the greatest long-term payoff.

When a student is dealing with a problem, or when her emotional state clearly indicates that something is bothering her, active listening is irreplaceable as a means of helping.

The Circle Session provides the opportunity for students to talk while others actively listen. By being given this opportunity, students gain important self-knowledge. Once they see that we do not intend to change them and that they may speak freely without threat of being "wrong," students find it easier to examine themselves and begin to see areas where they can make positive change in their lives. Just through the consistent process of sharing in a safe environment, students develop the ability to clarify their feelings and thoughts. They are encouraged to go deeper, find their own direction, and express and face strong feelings that may at other times be hidden obstacles to their growth. The important point is that students really can solve their own problems, develop self-awareness, and learn skills that will enable them to become responsible members of society if they are listened to effectively.

Awareness

Words are the only tool we have for systematically turning our attention and awareness to the feelings within us, and for describing and reflecting on our thoughts and behaviors. Feelings, after all, lead people to marry, to seek revenge, to launch war, to create great works of art, and to commit their lives to the service of others. They are vital and compelling.

For students to be able to manage their feelings, they must know what those feelings are. To know what they are, they must practice describing them in words. When a particular feeling is grasped in words several times, the mind soon begins to automatically recall ideas and concepts in association with the feeling and can start to provide ways of dealing with the feeling; e.g., "I'm feeling angry and I need to get away from this situation to calm down."

With practice, the mind becomes more and more adept at making these connections. When a recognized feeling comes up, the mind can sort through alternative responses to the feeling. As a student practices this response sequence in reaction to a variety of feelings, he will find words floating into consciousness that accurately identify what is going on emotionally and physically for him. This knowledge in turn develops the capacity to think before and during action. One mark of high emotional intelligence is the ability to recognize one's feelings and to take appropriate, responsible action. The lower a student's EQ, the more often emotional hijackings will determine her behavior. The ability to put words to feelings, to understand those words, to sort through an internal repertoire of responses and to choose appropriate, responsible behavior in reaction to a feeling indicates a high level of self-awareness and emotional intelligence.

By verbally exploring their own experiences in the circle and listening to others do the same, all in an environment of safety, students are gently and gradually prompted to explore deeper within themselves and to grow and expand in their understanding of others. As this mutual sharing takes place, they learn that feelings, thoughts, and behaviors are real and experienced by everyone. They see others succeeding and failing in the same kinds of ways they succeed and fail. They also begin to see each person as unique and to realize that they are unique, too. Out of this understanding, students experience a growing concern for others. A sense of responsibility develops as the needs, problems, values, and preferences of others penetrate their awareness.

Personal Mastery

Personal mastery can be defined as self-confidence together with responsible competence. Self-confidence is believing in oneself as a capable human being. Responsible competence is the willingness to take responsibility for one's actions coupled with the ability to demonstrate fundamental human relations skills (competencies).

Through participation in Circle Sessions, students are encouraged to explore their successes and hear positive comments about their efforts. Many Circle Session topics heighten students' awareness of their own successes and those of others. Failure, or falling short, is a reality that is also examined. The focus, however, is not to remind students that they have failed; instead these topics enable students to see that falling short is common and universal and is experienced by all people when they strive to accomplish things.

Circle Session topics often address human relations competencies, such as the ability to include others, assume and share responsibility, offer help, behave assertively, solve problems, resolve conflicts, etc. Such topics elevate awareness in the human relations domain and encourage students to more effectively exercise these competencies and skills each day. The first step in a student's developing any competency is knowing that he or she is capable of demonstrating it. The Circle Session is particularly adept at helping students to recognize and acknowledge their own capabilities.

A particularly important element of personal mastery is personal responsibility. By focusing on their positive behaviors and accomplishments, the attention of students is directed toward the internal and external rewards that can be gained when they behave responsibly.

The Circle Session is a wonderful tool for teaching cooperation. As equitably as possible, the circle structure attempts to meet the needs of all participants. Everyone's feelings are accepted. Comparisons and judgments are not made. The circle is not another competitive arena, but is guided by a spirit of collaboration. When students practice fair, respectful interaction with one another, they benefit from the experience and are likely to employ these responsible behaviors in other life situations.

Interpersonal Skills

Relating effectively to others is a challenge we all face. People who are effective in their social interactions have the ability to understand others. They know how to interact flexibly, skillfully, and responsibly. At the same time, they recognize their own needs and maintain their own integrity. Socially effective people can process the nonverbal as well as verbal messages of others. They possess the very important awareness that all people have the power to affect one another. They are aware of not only how others affect them, but the effects their behaviors have on others.

The Circle Session process has been designed so that healthy, responsible behaviors are modeled by the teacher or counselor in his or her role as circle leader. The rules also require that the students relate positively and effectively to one another. The Circle Session brings out and affirms the positive qualities inherent in everyone and allows students to practice

effective modes of communication. Because Circle Sessions provide a place where participants are listened to and their feelings accepted, students learn how to provide the same conditions to peers and adults outside the circle.

One of the great benefits of the Circle Session is that it does not merely teach young people about social interaction, it lets them interact! Every Circle Session is a real-life experience of social interaction where the students share, listen, explore, plan, dream, and problem solve together. As they interact, they learn about each other and they realize what it takes to relate effectively to others. Any given Circle Session may provide a dozen tiny flashes of positive interpersonal insight for an individual participant. Gradually, the reality of what constitutes effective behavior in relating to others is internalized.

Through this regular sharing of interpersonal experiences, the students learn that behavior can be positive or negative, and sometimes both at the same time. Consequences can be constructive, destructive, or both. Different people respond differently to the same event. They have different feelings and thoughts. The students begin to understand what will cause what to happen; they grasp the concept of cause and effect; they see themselves affecting others and being affected by others.

The ability to make accurate interpretations and responses in social interactions allows students to know where they stand with themselves and with others. They can tell what actions "fit" a situation. Circle Sessions are marvelous testing grounds where students can observe themselves and others in action, and can begin to see themselves as contributing to the good and bad feelings of others. With this understanding, students are helped to conclude that being responsible towards others feels good, and is the most valuable and personally rewarding form of interaction.

How to Set Up Circle Sessions

Group Size and Composition

Circle Sessions are a time for focusing on individuals' contributions in an unhurried fashion. For this reason, each circle group needs to be kept relatively small — eight to twelve usually works best. Once they move beyond the primary grades, students are capable of extensive verbalization. You will want to encourage this, and not stifle them because of time constraints.

Each group should be as heterogeneous as possible with respect to sex, ability, and racial/ethnic background. Sometimes there will be a group in which all the students are particularly reticent to speak. At these times, bring in an expressive student or two who will get things going. Sometimes it is necessary for practical reasons to change the membership of a group. Once established, however, it is advisable to keep a group as stable as possible.

Length and Location of Circles

Most circle sessions last approximately 20 to 30 minutes. At first students tend to be reluctant to express themselves fully because they do not yet know that the circle is a safe place. Consequently your first sessions may not last more than 10 to 15 minutes. Generally speaking, students become comfortable and motivated to speak with continued experience.

In middle-school classrooms circle sessions may be conducted at any time during the class period. Starting circle sessions at the beginning of the period allows additional time in case students become deeply involved in the topic. If you start circles late in the period, make sure the students are aware of their responsibility to be concise.

In elementary classes, any time of day is appropriate for Circle Sessions. Some teachers like to set the tone for the day by beginning with circles; others feel it's a perfect way to complete the day and to send the students away with positive feelings.

Circle sessions may be carried out wherever there is room for students to sit in a circle and experience few or no distractions. Most leaders prefer to have students sit in chairs rather than on the floor. Students seem to be less apt to invade one another's space while seated in chairs. Some leaders conduct sessions outdoors, with students seated in a secluded, grassy area.

How to Get Started

Teachers and counselors have used numerous methods to involve students in the circle process. What works well for one leader or class does not always work for another. Here are two basic strategies leaders have successfully used to get groups started. Whichever you use, we recommend that you post a chart listing the circle session rules and procedures to which every participant may refer.

1. Start one group at a time, and cycle through all groups. If possible, provide an opportunity for every student to experience a circle session in a setting where there are no disturbances. This may mean arranging for another staff member or aide to take charge of the students not participating in the circle. Non-participants may work on course work or silent reading, or, if you have a cooperative librarian, they may be sent to the library to work independently or in small groups on a class assignment. Repeat this procedure until all of the students have been involved in at least one circle session.

Next, initiate a class discussion about the circle sessions. Explain that from now on you will be meeting with each circle group in the classroom, with the remainder of the class present. Ask the students to help you plan established procedures for the remainder of the class to follow.

Meet with each circle session group on a different day, systematically cycling through the groups.

2. Combine inner and outer circles. Meet with one circle session group while another group listens and observes as an outer circle. Then have the two groups change places, with the students on the outside becoming the inner circle, and responding verbally to the topic. If you run out of time in middle-school classrooms, use two class periods for this. Later, a third group may be added to this alternating cycle. The end product of this arrangement is two or more groups (comprising everyone in the class) meeting together simultaneously. While one group is involved in discussion, the other groups listen and observe as members of an outer circle. Invite the members of the outer circle to participate in the review and discussion phases of the circle.

Managing the Rest of the Class

A number of arrangements can be made for students who are not participating in circle sessions. Here are some ideas:

- Arrange the room to ensure privacy. This may involve placing a circle of chairs or carpeting in a corner, away from other work areas. You might construct dividers from existing furniture, such as bookshelves or screens, or simply arrange chairs and tables in such a way that the circle area is protected from distractions.

- Involve aides, counselors, parents, or fellow teachers. Have an aide conduct a lesson with the rest of the class while you meet with a circle group. If you do not have an aide assigned to you, use auxiliary staff or parent volunteers.

- Have students work quietly on subject-area assignments in pairs or small, task-oriented groups.

- Utilize student aides or leaders. If the seat-work activity is in a content area, appoint students who show ability in that area as "consultants," and have them assist other students.

- Give the students plenty to do. List academic activities on the board. Make materials for quiet individual activities available so that students cannot run out of things to do and be tempted to consult you or disturb others.

- Make the activity of students outside the circle enjoyable. When you can involve the rest of the class in something meaningful to them, students will probably be less likely to interrupt the circle.

- Have the students work on an ongoing project. When they have a task in progress, students can simply resume where they left off, with little or no introduction from you. In these cases, appointing a "person in charge," "group leader," or "consultant" is wise.

- Allow individual journal-writing. While a circle is in progress, have the other students make entries in a private (or share-with-teacher-only) journal. The topic for journal writing could be the same topic that is being discussed in the Circle Session. Do not correct the journals but, if you read them, be sure to respond to the entries with your own written thoughts, where appropriate.

Leading the Circle Session

This section is a thorough guide for conducting Circle Sessions. It covers major points to keep in mind and answers questions which will arise as you begin using the program. Please remember that these guidelines are presented to assist you, not to restrict you. Follow them and trust your own leadership style at the same time.

Circle Session Procedures for the Leader

1. Setting up the circle (1-2 minutes)

2. Reviewing the ground rules (1-2 minutes) *

3. Introducing the topic (1-2 minutes)

4. Sharing by circle members (12-18 minutes)

5. Reviewing what is shared (3-5 minutes) **

6. Summary discussion (2-8 minutes)

7. Closing the circle (less than 1 minute)

*optional after the first few sessions

**optional

Introducing the topic (1-2 minutes)

State the topic in your own words. Elaborate and provide examples as each activity suggests. Add clarifying statements of your own that will help the students understand the topic. Answer questions about the topic, and emphasize that there are no "right" responses. Finally, restate the topic, opening the session to responses (theirs and yours). Sometimes taking your turn first helps the students understand the aim of the topic. At various points throughout the session, state the topic again.

Just prior to leading a circle session, contemplate the topic and think of at least one possible response that you can make during the sharing phase.

Setting up the circle (1-2 minutes)

As you sit down with the students in the circle, remember that you are not teaching a lesson. You are facilitating a group of people. Establish a positive atmosphere. In a relaxed manner, address each student by name, using eye contact and conveying warmth. An attitude of seriousness blended with enthusiasm will let the students know that the circle session is an important learning experience — an activity that can be interesting and meaningful.

Reviewing the ground rules (1-2 minutes).

At the beginning of the first session, and at appropriate intervals thereafter, go over the rules for the circle session. They are shown at the right.

From this point on, demonstrate to the students that you expect them to remember and abide by the ground rules. Convey that you think well of them and know they are fully capable of responsible behavior. Let them know that by coming to the session they are making a commitment to listen and show acceptance and respect for the other students and you.

Circle Session Rules

1. Bring yourself to the circle and nothing else.

2. Everyone gets a turn to share, including the leader.

3. You can skip your turn if you wish.

4. Listen to the person who is sharing.

5. The time is shared equally.

6. Stay in your own space.

7. There are no interruptions, probing, put-downs, or gossip.

Sharing by circle members (12-18 minutes)

The most important point to remember is this: The purpose of the circle session is to give students an opportunity to express themselves and be accepted for the experiences, thoughts, and feelings they share. Avoid taking the action away from the circle members. They are the stars!

Reviewing what is shared (optional 3-5 minutes)

Besides modeling effective listening (the very best way to teach it) and positively reinforcing students for attentive listening, a review can be used to deliberately improve listening skills in circle members.

Reviewing is a time for reflective listening, when circle members feed back what they heard each other say during the sharing phase of the circle. Besides encouraging effective listening, reviewing provides circle members with additional recognition. It validates their experience and conveys the idea, "you are important," a message we can all profit from hearing often.

To review, a circle member simply addresses someone who shared, and briefly paraphrases what the person said ("John, I heard you say....").

The first few times you conduct reviews, stress the importance of checking with the speaker to see if the review accurately summarized the main things that were shared. If the speaker says, "No," allow him or her to make corrections. Stress, too, the importance of speaking directly to the speaker, using the person's name and the pronoun "you," not "he" or "she." If someone says, "She said that...," intervene as promptly and respectfully as possible and say to the reviewer, "Talk to Betty...Say you." This is very important. The person whose turn is being reviewed will have a totally different feeling when talked *to*, instead of *about*.

Note: Remember that the review is optional and is most effective when used occasionally, not as a part of every circle.

Summary discussion (2-8 minutes)

The summary discussion is the cognitive portion of the circle session. During this phase, the leader asks thought-provoking questions to stimulate free discussion and higher-level thinking. Each circle session in this book includes summary questions; however, at times you may want to formulate questions that are more appropriate to the level of understanding in your group—or to what was actually shared in the circle. If you wish to make connections between the circle session topic and your content area, ask questions that will accomplish that objective and allow the summary discussion to extend longer.

It is important that you not confuse the summary with the review. The review is optional; the summary is not. The summary meets the need of people of all ages to find meaning in what they do. Thus, the summary serves as a necessary culmination to each circle session by allowing the students to clarify the key concepts they gained from the session.

Closing the circle (less than 1 minute).

The ideal time to end a circle session is when the summary discussion reaches natural closure. Sincerely thank everyone for being part of the circle. Don't thank specific students for speaking, as doing so might convey the impression that speaking is more appreciated than listening alone. Then close the circle by saying, "The circle session is over," or "OK, that ends our session."

More about Circle Session Procedures and Rules

The next few paragraphs offer further clarification concerning circle session leadership.

Why should students bring themselves to the circle and nothing else? Individual teachers differ on this point, but most prefer that students not bring objects (such as pencils, books, etc.) to the circle that may be distracting.

Who gets to talk? Everyone. The importance of acceptance in Circle Sessions cannot be overly stressed. In one way or another practically every ground rule says one thing: accept one another. When you model acceptance of students, they will learn how to be accepting. Each individual in the circle is important and deserves a turn to speak if he or she wishes to take it. Equal opportunity to become involved should be given to everyone in the circle.

Circle members should be reinforced equally for their contributions. There are many reasons why a leader may become more enthused over what one student shares than another. The response may be more on target, reflect more depth, be more entertaining, be philosophically more in keeping with one's own point of view, and so on. However, students need to be given equal recognition for their contributions, even if the contribution is to listen silently throughout the session.

In most of the circle sessions, plan to take a turn and address the topic, too. Students usually appreciate it very much and learn a great deal when their teachers and counselors are willing to tell about their own experiences, thoughts, and feelings. In this way you let your students know that you acknowledge your own humanness.

Does everyone have to take a turn? No. Students may choose to skip their turns. If the circle becomes a pressure situation in which the members are coerced in any way to speak, it will become an unsafe place where participants are not comfortable. Meaningful discussion is unlikely in such an atmosphere. By allowing students to make this choice, you are showing them that you accept their right to remain silent if that is what they choose to do.

As you begin circles, it will be to your advantage if one or more students decline to speak. If you are imperturbable and accepting when this happens, you let them know you are offering them an opportunity to experience something you think is valuable, or at least worth a try, and not attempting to force-feed them. You as a leader should not feel compelled to share a personal experience in every session, either. However, if you decline to speak in most of the sessions, this may have an inhibiting effect on the students' willingness to share.

A word should also be said about how this ground rule has sometimes been carried to extremes. Sometimes leaders have bent over backwards to let students know they don't have to take a turn. This seeming lack of enthusiasm on the part of the leader has caused reticence in the students. In order to avoid this outcome, don't project any personal insecurity as you lead the session. Be confident in your proven ability to work with students. Expect something to happen and it will.

Some circle leaders ask the participants to raise their hands when they wish to speak, while others simply allow free verbal sharing without soliciting the leader's permission first. Choose the procedure that works best for you, but do not call on anyone unless you can see signs of readiness.

Some leaders have reported that their first circles fell flat—that no one, or just one or two students, had anything to say. But they continued to have circles, and at a certain point everything changed. Thereafter, the students had a great deal to say that these leaders considered worth waiting for. It appears that in these cases the leaders' acceptance of the right to skip turns was a key factor. In time most students will contribute verbally when they have something they want to say, and when they are assured there is no pressure to do so.

Sometimes a silence occurs during a circle session. Don't feel you have to jump in every time someone stops talking. During silences students have an opportunity to think about what they would like to share or to contemplate an important idea they've heard. A general rule of thumb is to allow silence to the point that you observe group discomfort. At that point move on. Do not switch to another topic. To do so implies you will not be satisfied until the students speak. If you change to another topic, you are telling them you didn't really mean it when you said they didn't have to take a turn if they didn't want to.

If you are bothered about students who attend a number of circles and still do not share verbally, reevaluate what you consider to be involvement. Participation does not necessarily mean talking. Students who do not speak are listening and learning.

How can I encourage effective listening?

The Circle Session is a time (and place) for students and leaders to strengthen the habit of listening by doing it over and over again. No one was born knowing how to listen effectively to others. It is a skill like any other that gets better as it is practiced. In the immediacy of the circle session, the members become keenly aware of the necessity to listen, and most students respond by expecting it of one another.

In the Circle Session, listening is defined as the respectful focusing of attention on individual speakers. It includes eye contact with the speaker and open body posture. It eschews interruptions of any kind. When you conduct a circle session, listen and encourage listening in the students by (1) focusing your attention on the person who is speaking, (2) being receptive to what the speaker is saying (not mentally planning your next remark), and (3) recognizing the speaker when she finishes speaking, either verbally ("Thanks, Shirley") or nonverbally (a nod and a smile).

To encourage effective listening in the students, reinforce them by letting them know you have noticed they were listening to each other and you appreciate it. Occasionally conducting a review after the sharing phase also has the effect of sharpening listening skills.

How can I ensure the students get equal time?

When circle members share the time equally, they demonstrate their acceptance of the notion that everyone's contribution is of equal importance. It is not uncommon to have at least one dominator in a group. This person is usually totally unaware that by continuing to talk he or she is taking time from others who are less assertive.

Be very clear with the students about the purpose of this ground rule. Tell them at the outset how much time there is and whether or not you plan to conduct a review. When it is your turn, always limit your own contribution. If someone goes on and on, do intervene (dominators need to know what they are doing), but do so as gently and respectfully as you can.

What are some examples of put-downs?
Put-downs convey the message, "You are not okay as you are." Some put-downs are deliberate, but many are made unknowingly. Both kinds are undesirable in a Circle Session because they destroy the atmosphere of acceptance and disrupt the flow of discussion. Typical put-downs include:

- overquestioning.
- statements that have the effect of teaching or preaching
- advice giving
- one-upsmanship
- criticism, disapproval, or objections
- sarcasm
- statements or questions of disbelief

How can I deal with put-downs?
There are two major ways for dealing with put-downs in circle sessions: preventing them from occurring and intervening when they do.

Going over the ground rules with the students at the beginning of each session, particularly in the earliest sessions, is a helpful preventive technique. Another is to reinforce the students when they adhere to the rule. Be sure to use nonpatronizing, nonevaluative language.

Unacceptable behavior should be stopped the moment it is recognized by the leader. When you become aware that a put-down is occurring, do whatever you ordinarily do to stop destructive behavior in the classroom. If one student gives another an unasked-for bit of advice, say for example, "Jane, please give Alicia a chance to tell her story." To a student who interrupts say, "Ed, it's Sally's turn." In most cases the fewer words, the better — students automatically tune out messages delivered as lectures.

Sometimes students disrupt the group by starting a private conversation with the person next to them. Touch the offender on the arm or shoulder while continuing to give eye contact to the student who is speaking. If you can't reach the offender, simply remind him or her of the rule about listening. If students persist in putting others down during circle sessions, ask to see them at another time and hold a brief one-to-one conference, urging them to follow the rules. Suggest that they reconsider their membership in the circle. Make it clear that if they don't intend to honor the ground rules, they are not to come to the circle.

How can I keep students from gossiping?
Periodically remind students that using names and sharing embarrassing information is not acceptable. Urge the students to relate personally to one another, but not to tell intimate details of their lives.

What should the leader do during the summary discussion?
Conduct the summary as an open forum, giving students the opportunity to discuss a variety of ideas and accept those that make sense to them. Don't impose your opinions on the students, or allow the students to impose theirs on one another. Ask open-ended questions, encourage higher-level thinking, contribute your own ideas when appropriate, and act as a facilitator.

Bibliography and Resources

Armstrong, Thomas, *In Their Own Way: Discovering and Encouraging Your Child's Personal Learning Style*, Los Angeles: Jeremy P. Tarcher, Inc., 1987.

Arnold, William, W. and Plas, Jeanne M., *The Human Touch: Today's Most Unusual Program for Productivity and Profit*, New York: Wiley, 1993.

Berry, Diane. S. and Pennebaker, James W., "Nonverbal and Verbal Emotional Expression and Health," *Psychotherapy and Psychosomatics*, Vol 59, 1993.

Brody, Leslie R. and Hall, Judith A., "Gender and Emotion," *Handbook of Emotions*, New York: Guilford Press, 1993.

Caulfield, Joan and Jennings, Wayne, "Emotional Aspect of Brain Recognized," *Networker*, Winter 1996.

Cowan, David, *Taking Charge of Organizational Conflict*, Spring Valley, California: Innerchoice Publishing, 1995.

Davidson, Richard, *The Nature of Emotion: Fundamental Questions*, New York and Oxford: Oxford University Press, 1995.

Dreikers, Rudolf, *Psychodynamics and Counseling*, Chicago: Adler School of Professional Psychology, 1967.

Evans, Phil, *Motivation and Emotion*, London: Routledge, 1989.

Francis, Martha E. and Pennebaker, James W., "Talking and Writing as Illness Prevention." *Medicine, Exercise, Nutrition and Health*, American Journal of Health Promotion, Vol. 6, Issue 4, 1992.

Gardner, Howard, *Frames of Mind: The Theory of Multiple Intelligences*, New York: Basic Books, 1983.

Goleman, Daniel, *Emotional Literacy: A Field Report*, Fetzer Institute of Dalamazoo, Michigan, 1996.

Goleman, Daniel, "Emotional Intelligence: Why It Can Matter More Than IQ," *Learning*, May/June, 1996.

Goleman, Daniel, *Emotional Literacy: Why It Can Matter More Than IQ*, New York: Bantam, 1995.

Humphry, Nicholas, *A History of the Mind: Evolution and the Birth of Consciousness*, New York: Simon and Schuster, 1992.

Lazarus, Richard S., *Passion and Reason: Making Sense of Our Emotions*, New York and Oxford: Oxford Universaity Press, 1994.

Levenson, Robert W, "Human Emotion: A Functional View," *The Nature of Emotion: Fundamental Questions*, Oxford University Press, 1995.

Ralston, Faith, *Hidden Dynamics: How Emotions Affect Business Performance*, New York: American Management Association, 1995.

Richards, Dick, *Artful Work: Awakening Joy, Meaning, and Commitment in the Workplace*, San Francisco: Berrett-Koehler Publishers, 1995.

Saarni, Carolyn, "Emotional Competence: How Emotions and Relationships Become Integrated," in Thompson, R.A., *Socioemtional Development*, Lincoln and London: University of Nebraska Press, 1990.

Salovey, Peter, and Mayer, John D., "Emotional Intelligence," *Imagination, Cognition, and Personality 9*, 1990.

Solomon, Robert C., *The Passions: Emotions and the Meaning of Life*, Indianapolis and Cambridge: Hacket Publishing Company, 1993.

Vail, Priscilla, "The On Off Switch for Learning," *Connections: The Newletter of Social and Emotional Learning*, Collaborative for the Advancement of Social and Emotional Learning, Yale University, 1994.

Self-Awareness

Activities in this unit teach students to:

- recognize and describe their own worth and worthiness.

- identify characteristics about themselves that they convey to others

- describe what is going on inside of themselves physically, emotionally, and mentally.

Circle Sessions in this unit allow students to:

- disclose something about themselves that they feel positive about.

- describe a place they enjoy being and how that place affects them emotionally.

The First Time I . . .
Dyads and Discussion

Objectives:
The students will:
—recognize and describe their own worth and worthiness.
—define self physically, emotionally, socially, and intellectually.
—identify strengths, talents, and special abilities in self and others.
—practice methods of positive self-talk.

Materials:
the dyad topics (below) listed on the chalkboard

Procedure:
Have the students form dyads and sit facing each other. Announce that the students are going to take turns talking to each other about a series of topics. In your own words, explain: *Each person will have two minutes to speak to the topic while the other person listens. The person talking should try to be as open as she or he can comfortably be. The person listening should be as good a listener as possible, focusing on the speaker rather than paying attention to other things in the room or to personal thoughts. The listener must not interrupt the speaker for any reason during this dyad sequence.*

Begin the sequence with the first topic and call time after 2 minutes. Have the students switch roles and address the same topic again. Follow the same procedure for the remaining topics.

Ask the students to stand up and mill around the room, making contact with at least four students. Tell them that each time they make contact, they are to briefly state one thing they learned from the dyad sequence.

Have the students return to their seats and lead a debriefing discussion. Ask these and other questions:

Discussion questions:
1. How much risk is involved in doing something for the first time?
2. What determines the level of risk involved in a behavior or activity?
3. What is the relationship between risk level and your feelings of accomplishment?
4. What do we gain be recalling accomplishments in this way?

Dyad Topics:
"The First Time I. . .
. . .Got a Job"
. . .Said 'No' to Someone"
. . .Decided to Do Something I Thought Was Important"
. . .Stood Up for My Rights"
. . .Talked to a Group of People"
. . .Tried Out for a Position, Team, Club, or Group"
. . .Spoke Up for My Beliefs"

A Self-Portrait
Art Experience and Discussion

Objective:
The students will identify and illustrate characteristics about themselves that they want to convey to others.

Materials:
various art supplies, like paints, charcoal, colored pencils, paper, etc.; collage materials, such as scissors, glue, tape, old magazines, photos, etc.

Procedure:
Explain to the students that you would like them to portray their self-image artistically. Urge them to select any art form that they would like to use to express themselves, e.g., charcoal for sketching, collage, painting, finger paints, and so forth. Stress that they may creatively show as many facets of themselves as they like, in anything from a simple sketch of their face to a complex collage that integrates many aspects of themselves.

Discussions questions:
Allow the students to exhibit their works, pass them around, or keep them, as you/ they choose. Facilitate a discussion, asking these and other relevant questions:
1. What did you learn about yourself by doing your self-portrait?
2. Do you think someone would know you better by looking at your self-portrait? In what ways?
3. What do you see when you look at your self-portrait as if it were of someone else? ...by someone else?

Extension:
Either before or after this activity, duplicate and hand out to each student a copy of the experience sheet, "Looking At My Many Selves."

Variation:
Have the students complete their self-portrait outside of class. Begin the activity by sharing and discussing the portraits.

Looking At My Many Selves
Experience Sheet

There is a part of me that wants to write , a part that wants to theorize, a part that wants to sculpt, a part that wants to teach . . . To force myself into a single role, to decide to be just one thing in life, would kill off large parts of me. Rather, I recognize that I live now and only now, and I will do what I want to do this moment and not what I decided was best for me yesterday.

This is what a man named Hugh Prather had to say about himself in a book he wrote called *Notes to Myself.*

Have you ever noticed how much people can change from time to time — even you? It's as if there are a lot of people inside each one of us. We all have many parts. There are sad parts, happy parts, clown parts and serious parts, pretty parts and ugly parts, smart parts and dumb parts, child parts and parent parts, and adult parts, parts that study and learn, parts that play and laugh, dozens of parts. Take a look at some of your parts. Finish these sentences with as many endings as you can. These are some of the people <u>you</u> are at different times.

Sometimes I like to _____

Sometimes I remind myself of _____

Sometimes I try to be _____

Sometimes I am _____

Here is another way to look at the parts that make up you. At the top of each column put down a word that describes you because of something you do. It might be student, son or daughter, friend, athlete, cook, or whatever. Next, list some of the things you do when you are in that role. Suppose you choose "cook" as your title. You might list recipe reader, organizer, creator or taster, timer, or even dishwasher. Give it a try.

1. _____ **2.** _____ **3.** _____

_____ _____ _____

_____ _____ _____

_____ _____ _____

_____ _____ _____

_____ _____ _____

Was it hard at times to figure out some of your parts? Keep in mind that most people have a hard time looking at some parts of themselves. There are parts we like and parts we don't like. That's natural and human. It helps to know all about ourselves, even if it's hard sometimes. Then we can take full charge of ourselves and change ourselves if we decide to.

You've looked at some of your parts. Now take a close look at who YOU are. Finish these statements with the first words that come to mind. There's no need to take a long time thinking about each one unless you really want to. Don't worry about truth or falsehood or whether they make sense. Just have a good time looking at YOU.

I feel happiest when _____

_____

_____

I am sad when _____

_____

_____

I wonder if I _____

_____

_____

I trust _____

_____

_____

It hurts me when _____

_____

_____

I get angry when _____

_____

_____

I feel satisfied when _____

_____

_____

I feel most loved when _____

_____

_____

Did you like doing this exercise? Parts of it might have been easy and enjoyable, while other parts might have been hard. Were there some items that were tough to complete? That's okay. What you might do now is go back to those hard ones and look at them again. See if rethinking them helps.

Getting More in Touch with Me
A Guided Awareness Exercise

Objectives:
The students will:
—develop greater awareness.
—experience and describe what is going on inside of them physically, emotionally, and mentally.

Procedure:
Tell the students that you would like to do a guided-awareness exercise with them that will help them focus on themselves and sharpen their self-awareness. Then, read the following very slowly in a relaxed, clear tone. Allow plenty of time (at least five seconds) between images. Following the exercise, facilitate a class discussion focusing on the experience.

Get comfortable in your chair and relax your body...Close your eyes and allow whatever images enter your mind to pass through...Just take a look at them...Don't do anything about them...Be aware of the position of your body...How does the chair feel against your back and underneath you?...Feel the chair supporting you...Make yourself as heavy in the chair as you can...Feel the weight of your feet on the floor...Be aware of the space around you...Feel the temperature of the air... Feel your tongue against the roof of your mouth...Be aware of the taste in your mouth...Be aware of the temperature of the air as it enters your nose...and as you exhale...Be aware of any muscle tension in your shoulders...upper body...lower body...legs...arms...Be aware of the feelings in your throat...and in your stomach.

Now be aware of your emotions...What are your feelings?...Are you sad? ...happy?

...curious? ...Or maybe you have no special feelings right now...What are you feeling?...Where do you feel emotions in your body? What is the location?...Be aware of what area in your body each feeling covers...What shape is your feeling?...Is it moving?...If so, what kind of movement is it?...What color is your feeling?...Has it changed?...What emotion are you feeling now?...Where is it exactly in your body?

Now, become aware of what you are thinking...What thoughts are coming into your head?...Just notice them...and then let them go as though they were a flowing stream...Now take a couple of minutes to notice some more of your thoughts. (Pause for about two minutes.)

Now be aware of what you are doing ...Are you moving? ...twitching? ...smiling? ...frowning? ...thinking?...relaxing?...What are you doing?

Now, keeping your eyes closed, gently come back into the room and become aware of the space around you...Picture the room you are about to open your eyes in...the walls...the floor...and all the other parts of the room...Gently and slowly open your eyes and look at the room and the people in it as though you are seeing them for the first time...What comes into your awareness?

Discussion questions:
1. What are some of the things that came into your awareness during the exercise?
2. What emotions did you feel? Where in your body were they located?
3. How do you feel now?

Something I Enjoy Doing That I Do Well
A Circle Session

Objective:

The students will share positive things about themselves with one another.

Introduce the Topic:

Say to the students: *In this session, we are going to talk about things we like to do and brag a little bit in the process. The topic is "Something I Enjoy Doing That I Do Well." So take a moment to think about something that you are good at, that you would feel OK telling the group about. Perhaps it's something you do away from school that none of us could know about unless you told us, or it could be something you are accomplishing in one of your classes. Tell us about anything that you like to do and do well.*

Don't be bashful about admitting that you do something well, because we already know that you've got talents and abilities. Everyone does. In this session, you have permission to talk about them. Think for a moment, If you don't feel like talking, just listen; that's fine, too. The topic is "Something I Enjoy Doing That I Do Well."

Discussion questions:

After the students have finished sharing, encourage them to talk about what they learned. Ask these and other questions:

1. How did you feel about describing what you do well?
2. Do you think it's OK to do things just for fun, or should everything we do be productive?
3. Did you learn anything that you didn't know before about someone in the circle?

A Favorite Place of Mine
A Circle Session

Objectives:

The students will:

—describe a place they enjoy being.

—discuss how preferences make each person unique.

Introduce the Topic:

Say to the students: *Our topic for this circle session is a very enjoyable one because it encourages us to talk about ourselves and the things we like. The topic is, "A Favorite Place of Mine." So give that some thought.*

Where do you really enjoy being? Perhaps an exciting place comes to mind, or one that's peaceful and beautiful. Maybe the most important thing about a place is who is there with you. Or perhaps when you think of a favorite place you usually focus on feeling relaxed or inspired. The place that comes to mind might be one you've seen in a picture or movie, but haven't yet visited. It might even be an imaginary place. Think about it for a few moments. The topic is, "A Favorite Place of Mine."

Discussion questions:

1. Did you notice any similarities in the places we mentioned and why we like those places?
2. How do your surroundings affect your mood? ...your thoughts?
3. Why do we depend on familiar surroundings?
4. What kind of person regularly seeks new and different surroundings?

Additional Circle Session Topics

A Person I Admire
A Secret Wish I Have
Something I Like to Do Alone
The Craziest Dream I Ever Had
One Way I Wish I Could Be Different
Something I Want to Keep
Something I Like to Do with Others
When I Felt Comfortable Just Being Me
Something I Need Help With
My Idea of a Perfect Saturday Afternoon
Something About My Culture That I Appreciate
The Funniest Thing That Ever Happened to Me
My Favorite Vacation
Something I Like to Do With My Family
My Favorite Daydream
One of the Best Things That Ever Happened to Me
My Favorite Possession
Something I Really Like to Do
A Friend of Mine Who Is Different From Me
Something I Really Like to Do at School
If I Had One Wish It Would Be
One Way I Wish I Could Be Different
One Thing I Am Sure I Can Do Well
Something I Want
A Special Occasion or Holiday Related to My Culture
A Person I'd Like to Be Like

Managing Feelings

Activities in this unit teach students to:

- differentiate between thoughts, feelings and behaviors, and learn how thoughts affect feelings, and feelings affect behavior.

- identify strategies for dealing with areas of personal discomfort.

- describe strategies for releasing negative feelings and managing negative moods.

Circle Sessions in this unit allow students to:

- describe incidents in which they handled their emotions well and discuss the mental processes that contributed to their success.

- understand the value of positive self talk.

Thoughts, Feelings, and Behaviors
Experience Sheet and Discussion

Objectives:

The students will:
—differentiate between thoughts, feelings, and behaviors.
—state that negative feelings are triggered by negative thoughts.

Materials:

index cards labeled with thought, feeling, or behavior words; one copy of the experience sheet, "Make Your Feelings Work for You," for each student

Procedures:

Distribute two or three index cards to each student. Prepare these cards in advance by labeling them with various thought, feeling, and behavior words, as shown:

Talk about the differences between thoughts, feelings, and behaviors. Give a few examples and ask the group as a whole to name the category to which each belongs. Then have the students take turns reading their cards aloud, identifying the appropriate category. Continue until the students appear to have grasped the concept.

Distribute the experience sheets. Give the students about 15 minutes to complete the sheet. Then ask them to form small groups and share what they have written. Conclude the activity with a class discussion.

Thoughts

remembering	reasoning
thinking	questioning
figuring	concentrating
forgetting	calculating
pondering	projecting

Feelings

joy	delight
anger	worry
fear	loneliness
depression	apathy
surprise	curiosity

Behaviors

running	kissing
talking	discussing
dancing	studying
playing	arguing
watching TV	working

Discussion Questions:

1. How do thoughts affect feelings? How do feelings affect behavior?
2. When you have feelings that you can't explain, does that mean that they have nothing to do with your thoughts? Explain.
3. How can we control our feelings? ...our thoughts?
4. When you have feelings that you think might be affecting your health, what can you do about them?
5. Can other people ever *make* you feel a certain way? Why or why not?

Make Your Feelings Work For You!
Experience Sheet

Our feelings help us function in many ways. For example, have you ever become frightened and, because of your fear, done something to protect yourself from a real danger? If so, your feelings caused you to take positive action.

Below is a list of feeling words. Pick one or two of them, and see if you can briefly explain how that emotion affects your behavior. How does it work for you?

anger	joy	power	patience
eagerness	indecisiveness	satisfaction	love
fatigue	protectiveness	pain	hope
courage	silliness	curiosity	

_____

_____

Now think about the emotions of self-pity, greed, jealousy, and possessiveness. **How do they affect behavior? What kinds of problems can they cause?**

_____

_____

Feelings have an effect on your body. They can wound and they can heal. Feelings can get "locked in" to your body when you refuse to accept and deal with them. This is a type of stress, and when it happens, real sickness can result. **Do you remember a time when you or someone else got sick under pressure? How about a stomachache or headache just before a test?**

_____

Sometimes feelings show in the form of a twitch or tic in a muscle; other times as a tight jaw or lost voice. **Below is a list of body reactions. Next to each one, list feelings that you think can lead to these body reactions.**

Tears _____   Smile _____

Lump in throat _____   Pounding heart _____

Sweaty palms _____   Clenched fists _____

Shaky arms and legs _____   Bouncy walk _____

Red face _____   Tight stomach _____

Frown _____   Trembling jaw _____

Squeaky voice _____   Slouched posture _____

Here are some things to try:

Get rid of old guilt feelings you may still have about something you did. The best way might be to go to the person or people you wronged, admit it, and apologize. If that isn't possible, imagine the situation. Replay it in your mind, doing what you wish you had done the first time.

Affirm yourself. People tend to like people who like themselves. You might feel ridiculous doing this, but give it a try anyway. Look in the mirror and say the nicest things you can think of to yourself _in a sincere way_. Establish a relationship with yourself as your very best friend, the person you can always count on to be on _your_ side.

Handling Discomfort
Experience Sheet and Discussion

Objectives:
Group members will:
—identify individual situations and personal characteristics that cause them discomfort.
—describe strategies for dealing with areas of discomfort.

Materials:
one copy of the experience sheet, "Things That Bother Me," for each student

Procedure:
Tell the students that they are going to have a chance to talk about ways of dealing with situations and problems that cause them particular discomfort.

Distribute the experience sheet and give the students a few minutes to complete it. Invite volunteers to share one or two items that they circled on their sheet. Model reflective listening, allowing the contributions of the students to generate discussion. Make these points:
- We are all bothered by different things because each of us is unique. We have different abilities, disabilities, likes, dislikes, perceptions and experiences.
- Everyone in the group is at the same stage of development, so we share common experiences and concerns.
- Talking about our discomforts and concerns can help us deal with them more effectively.

Discussion questions:
1. How many of the things you marked on your list can you change?
2. In your opinion, how many kids are bothered by the same things you are?
3. What feelings do you have in connection with the things that bother you?
4. When you have a problem, how do you usually resolve it?
5. How can you handle the stress that is caused by your discomfort?

Things That Bother Me
Experience Sheet

Read the list carefully and put a check next to any problems that bother you. If you are having a problem that is *not* on the list, describe it at the bottom.

I am uncomfortable because I/I am...

1. ...shorter than the other kids.
2. ...taller than the other kids.
3. ...have a speech impairment.
4. ...lose my temper; get into fights.
5. ...don't like school.
6. ...have too much work to do at home.
7. ...timid or shy.
8. ...don't know how to act at parties.
9. ...disliked by other kids.
10. ...talked about behind my back by other kids.
11. ...teased by other kids.
12. ...afraid to try new things.
13. ...don't like my teacher.
14. ...afraid of someone at home.
15. ...too fat.
16. ...too thin.
17. ...not smart enough.
18. ...don't have anyone to talk to at home.
19. ...have no place to study at home.
20. ...have a disability.
21. ...don't read well.
22. ...don't understand math.
23. ...afraid to admit my mistakes.
24. ...don't have nice clothes.
25. ...hungry all the time.
26. ...chosen last for teams.
27. ...not having any fun at school.
28. ...disliked by my teacher.
29. ...have bad dreams.
30. ...lose things.
31. ...have almost no friends.
32.
33.
34.

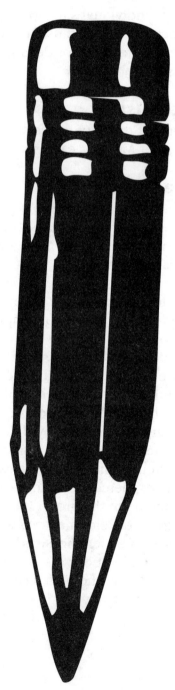

Managing Moods
Experience Sheet and Discussion

Objectives:

Group members will:

—explain how moods are affected by feelings left over from conflicts.

—identify problems and feelings associated with specific conflicts.

—describe strategies for releasing residual feelings and managing negative moods.

Materials:

one copy of the experience sheet, "Three Lousy Moods," for each student; chalkboard or chart paper; 3" x 5" index cards

Procedure:

Begin by asking the group: *Have you ever been in an extremely bad mood because of something negative that happened in one relatively small area of your life ?*

Invite volunteers to briefly share their "bad mood" experiences. Then, ask for a show of hands from students who have behaved badly toward a friend or family member for no particular reason other than they were in a bad mood. Point out that this sort of thing happens all the time.

Distribute the experience sheets and quickly go over the directions. Allow the students to work two's or three's to complete the sheet. Allow about 10 minutes.

Take a few minutes to discuss the three scenarios described on the experience sheet. Looking at one scenario at a time, ask the students how they answered the questions. Help the students recognize and describe how Ahmad, Rita, and Mike each started with a specific problem or conflict which produced certain feelings (frustration, worry, disappointment, anxiety, embarrassment, etc.). In all three cases, these first feelings were followed by anger, and the anger carried over into unrelated activities involving unsuspecting friends.

Write the following guidelines on the board:

GUIDE TO MANAGING MOODS

1. BUY YOURSELF SOME TIME!!!!!

2. Fill this time with mood management strategies.

3. It takes time for feelings to go away naturally. Don't let them affect other activities.

Ask the students: *Why is it so important to "buy time" when you are experiencing negative feelings associated with a problem or conflict?*

Facilitate a discussion around the three guidelines, inviting input and examples from the students, and making these points:

- The feelings we take away from a conflict (residual feelings) tend to stay with us for some time. Even a well-managed conflict is stressful, and left over feelings carry over into other activities and relationships. In addition, they can be hard on us physically.

- Internal conflicts, or conflicts that cannot be immediately resolved for one reason or another, also produce stress. Negative feelings may be with us constantly until the problem is resolved.

- Residual feelings and feelings associated with unresolved conflict affect our moods.

- The use of *mood-management strategies* can help us relieve stress and negative feelings, lessening the chance that a "bad mood" will result in damage to our body, our relationships, and other areas of our life.

On the board, write the heading, "**Mood Management Strategies**." Ask the students to help you brainstorm positive, healthy ways of releasing anger and other negative feelings. List all ideas. Include items such as:

- Talk with a trusted friend or adult.
- Run laps around the block or track.
- Leave the situation and take several slow, deep breaths.
- Get something to eat or drink.
- Listen to relaxing music.
- Take a walk in a pleasant natural setting.
- Imagine being in a favorite place.
- Work on a project or hobby.

Give each student a 3" x 5" card. Suggest that the students write down three or four mood management ideas that they think might work for them. Encourage them to carry the card with them, or tape it to a mirror or closet door at home as a reminder.

In subsequent sessions, ask volunteers to report on their progress using mood management strategies. Frequently remind the students that these strategies are short-term controls, not permanent solutions to big problems. However, they do relieve stress and allow us to enter into problem solving and conflict resolution with greater self-control and productivity.

Three Lousy Moods
Experience Sheet

Read the following scenarios. Write your answers to the questions on the other side of the sheet.

Scenario 1:

Ahmad was just finishing a report on the computer when he hit the wrong key and erased all of his work. He felt totally frustrated and starting to get angry with himself, but he had to get to his next class. Ahmad walked out of the computer room and down the hall. Lost in his thoughts about doing something so stupid, he stumbled right into Judy , knocking her books all over the floor. Then he gave her a disgusted look and yelled, "Why don't you look where you're going."

Discussion questions:

1. What was Ahmad's real problem?
2. What were his first feelings about that problem?
3. What were some of his other feelings?
4. What did Judy do that caused Ahmad to behave toward her the way he did?
5. Why did Ahmad yell at Judy?

Scenario 2:

Rita was ready to leave for school, but she couldn't find her books and nobody seemed to know where they were. She had two assignments due that day and both were inside her books. She started to get upset. After nearly thirty minutes of searching, Rita found the books in one of her little sister, Martha's, favorite hiding places. When she confronted her, Martha admitted hiding them. Even though she found her books, Rita was still mad at her sister and left for school late and in a terrible mood. When she walked into her first class, her best friend Cathy said, "Hi girl, you look upset." Rita snapped, "Leave me alone, I don't want to talk to you!"

Discussion questions:

1. What was Rita's real problem?
2. What were her first feelings about that problem?
3. What were some of her other feelings?
4. What did Cathy do that caused Rita to respond the way she did?
5. Why did Rita snap at Cathy?

Scenario 3:

Mike just found out that he didn't make the final cut for the basketball team. As he walked away from the gym, he started feeling angry. Mike thought it was unfair that some of the guys who did make the team couldn't shoot or maneuver nearly as well as he could. He felt crummy. When he walked around the corner, Mike saw a bunch of his friends talking. When Charlie saw Mike, he said, "What are you looking so down about?" Mike was embarrassed. He didn't want anyone to know he'd been cut, so all he said was, "None of your business," and walked off.

Discussion questions:

1. What was Mike's real problem?
2. What were his first feelings about that problem?
3. What were some of his other feelings?
4. What did Charlie do that caused Mike to behave the way he did?
5. Why was Mike rude to his friends, and why did he just walk off?

It Was Difficult, but I Controlled Myself
A Circle Session

Objective:

To allow students to explore times in their lives when their ability to use rational self control overruled the need to react impulsively and, therefore, reinforce their awareness and ability to manage impulses.

Introduce the Topic:

In your own words, say to the students: *The topic for today's session is "It Was Difficult, but I Controlled Myself." See if you can remember a time when you didn't want to, but you controlled yourself. You may have been about to react strongly to some situation without giving your behavior much thought, but were able to gain control of yourself. It might have been a time when someone else said or did something that was very upsetting, but you didn't let it get to you. Maybe you felt you were being treated unfairly or perhaps it was something like being left out of an activity or game. Think it over for a minute and remember not to share any names, just the incident. The topic for this session is "It Was Difficult, but I Controlled Myself."*

Discussion questions:

1. How did you feel about yourself when you were able to use self-control?
2. Sometimes we make things worse when we say or do something that makes us feel better at the moment. How can we judge when it's best to say or do what we feel like doing, and when its best to use self-control and hold ourselves back?
3. What are some of the things we can do to maintain self-control during a difficult time?

I Succeeded Because I Encouraged Myself
A Circle Session

Objective:
To help students understand the value of positive self-talk and that doubts are natural but can be overcome if we counteract them with encouraging words.

Introduce the Topic:
In your own words, say to the students:
Our topic for this session is, "I Succeeded Because I Encouraged Myself." Have you ever wanted to do something and weren't quite sure you could? Think of a time when you felt unsure, but encouraged yourself and, consequently, found a way to be successful. Perhaps you tried to teach your pet a trick, or needed to do a good job on a report for school. Maybe you were trying to master something on a computer, or were learning a new game. Whatever it was, you were not sure you could do it, but after giving yourself some encouraging words, you were successful. Take a few quiet moments to think it over. The topic is, "I Succeeded Because I Encouraged Myself."

Discussion questions:
1. What do you think caused each of you to be successful?
2. What kinds of doubts did you have to overcome to be successful?
3. What do you think would have happened if you had used discouraging words instead of encouraging words?

Additional Circle Session Topics

A Place Where I Feel Serene and at Peace
One of My Favorite Possessions
The Funniest Thing That Ever Happened to Me
My Idea of a Perfect Saturday Afternoon
One of the Best Things That Ever Happened to Me
A Secret Fear I Have
A Significant Event In My Life
Something I Feel Very Strongly About
A Time I Stood Up For Something I Strongly Believe In
Something I Hate to Do
Something I Love to Do
When I Felt Comfortable Just Being Me
Something I Like About Myself Right Now
I Did Something That Made Me Feel Like A Good Person
How I Feel About War
How I React When I'm Angry
Something I Did That Helped Someone Feel Good
How Somebody Hurt My Feelings
Something In My Life I'm Happy About
I Could Have Hurt Someone's Feelings, but I Didn't
A Feeling of Sadness I Remember
A Time I Felt Totally Alive and Interested In Something
A Feeling I Had a Hard Time Accepting
A Favorite Feeling
A Thought I Have That Makes Me Happy

Decision Making

Activities in this unit teach students to:

- develop and practice a process for effective decision making.

- explore possible outcomes and consequences of specific decisions.

- recognize that the consequences of decisions can be far reaching.

Circle Sessions in this unit allow students to:

- describe what it is like to make a decision that is based on sound judgment.

- explore feeling and thought processes involved in making a personal decision.

Decisions, Decisions!
Experience Sheet and Discussion

Objectives:

The students will:

—understand and describe how decisions are influenced.

—develop and practice a process for effective decision making.

Materials:

the experience sheet, "The Decision-Making Process," chalkboard or chart paper

Procedure:

Distribute the experience sheets. Read through the decision-making steps with the students, examining each one. Here are some suggestions to discuss and questions to ask:

- **(Step 2)** Knowing what is important to you and what you want to accomplish involves such things as likes/dislikes, values, and interests. Most important, it involves having goals. As the Cheshire Cat said to Alice: " If you don't know where you're going, any road will take you there."

- **(Step 3)** You can get information by talking to people, visiting places, watching TV, and reading. Once you have the information, you must be able to evaluate it. If two people tell you to do opposite things, how are you going to know which is right? What if neither is right? What if both are right?

- **(Step 5)** Look into the future. Ask yourself what would be the probable outcome if you chose each of the alternatives available. Practice with the students by asking them to predict their future based on these questions:

What would happen if:

- —you did not go to college?
- —you never got married?
- —you dropped out of school?
- —you became temporarily disabled?
- —you became a professional rock singer?
- —you decided never to drink alcohol?
- —you decided not to have children?
- —you became permanently disabled?

The Decision-Making Process
Experience Sheet

The decision-making process involves using what you know (or can learn) to get what you want.

Here are some steps to follow when you have a decision to make:
1. Recognize and define the decision to be made.
2. Know what is important to you—your values—and what you want to accomplish—your goal.
3. Study the information you have already; obtain and study new information, too.
4. List all of your alternatives.
5. List the advantages and disadvantages of each alternative.
6. Make a decision.
7. Develop a plan for carrying out your decision.

Now let's see how the process really works.
Think of a decision that you need to make in the next month. Define it here:

_____

_____

What is your goal relative to this decision?

_____

What kinds of things that are important in your life (your values) might affect, or be affected by, this decision?

_____

_____

_____

What kinds of information do you have or need?

Things to think about: _____   **Things to read:** _____

_____   _____

_____   _____

People to talk to: _____   **Things to do:** _____

_____   _____

_____   _____

What are your alternatives and what are the advantages and disadvantages of each?

Alternative	
Advantages	**Disadvantages**
Alternative	
Advantages	**Disadvantages**
Alternative	
Advantages	**Disadvantages**

Decision Point!

Which alternative has the best chance of producing the outcome you want?

Now that you've made a decision, you need to develop a plan for putting that decision into action. Use the space below to describe each step you need to take.

This Is the Plan

Steps:	When?
1.	
2.	
3.	
4.	
5.	
6.	

Decisions and Outcomes
Assessment and Discussion

Objectives:
The students will:
— understand and describe how decisions are influenced.
— state the outcomes and possible consequences of specific decisions.

Materials:
the experience sheet, "More About Decisions...," chalkboard or chart paper

Procedure:
Begin by defining *decision making* as a process in which a person selects from two or more choices. Point out that:

- A decision is not necessary unless there is more than one course of action to consider.
- *Not* deciding is making a decision.
- Two people facing similar decisions create unique outcomes because they want different things.
- Learning decision-making skills increases the possibility that a person can have what he or she wants.
- Each decision is limited by what a person is *able* to do and what he or she is *willing* to do. *Ability* is increased by having more alternatives. *Willingness* is usually determined by values and goals.

Ask the students to turn in their workbooks to the experience sheet, "More About Decisions." Give them a few minutes to complete the sheet.

To reinforce the differences between decisions and outcomes, play a game with the students. Introduce the game by saying: *I'm going to play a game of chance with you. You must make the decision whether or not to play. I am going to flip a coin. Before I flip it, I want you to write down on a slip of paper whether the coin is "heads" or "tails." Put your name on your paper, and give it to me. After I flip the coin, I will go through the papers and give every student who guessed correctly five extra points for the day. Those who guessed incorrectly will get no extra points. Remember, you do not have to play.*

Play the game. Afterwards, ask the students these questions:
— How many chose to play the game?
— How many chose not to play the game?
— If you chose to play the game, but guessed incorrectly, was that a poor decision or a poor outcome? (outcome)
— If you played the game and guessed correctly, was that a good decision or a good outcome? (both)
— If you chose not to play the game, was that a good or a poor decision? Why?

Conclude the activity with further discussion.

Discussion questions:
1. What did you find out about your "worst decision" from this activity?
2. What is the difference between decisions and outcomes?
3. If your decision was truly bad, how could you have made a better one?
4. What kinds of decisions require study and thought?

More About Decisions . . .
Experience Sheet

Write down all the decisions that you can remember making so far today. For example, you probably made decisions about what to wear, what to eat, how to spend your breaks and with whom. You may have made decisions about whether to go to class, how to approach an assignment, what to say to someone, and whether to tell the truth. Include all types of decisions on your list.

Decisions

1. _____

2. _____

3. _____

4. _____

5. _____

6. _____

7. _____

8. _____

9. _____

Now go back through your list of decisions and code each one with a number from this scale.

0 = I have no control over this type of decision; it is dictated by others.

1 = This type of decision is automatic, routine, or habitual.

2 = I occasionally think about this type of decision.

3 = I think about this type of decision, but I don't study it.

4 = I study this type of decision somewhat.

5 = I study this type of decision a lot.

What does this exercise tell you about how you make most of your decisions?

_____

_____

_____

_____

_____

_____

_____

What is the worst decision you ever made? Write a brief description of it:

_____

_____

_____

_____

_____

_____

_____

Decision or Outcome?   Next time you're tempted to kick yourself over a "bad" decision, consider this:

♣ When you say that a decision is poor, you probably mean the *result* or *outcome* is not what you wanted.

♣ Good decision making minimizes the possibility of getting bad outcomes, but it doesn't eliminate the possibility.

♣ A *decision* is the act of choosing among several possibilities based on your judgments.

♣ An *outcome* is the result, consequence, or aftermath of the decision.

♣ You have direct control over the decision, but *not* over the outcome.

♣ A good decision does not guarantee a good outcome, but it does increase the chances of a good outcome.

Go back and look at your "worst" decision again. Was it really a bad decision, or was it a reasonable decision with a bad outcome?

People Are Remembered for Their Decisions
Research and Discussion

Objective:

The students will identify and evaluate decisions of consequence made by historical or contemporary figures.

Procedure:

Tell the class about a well-known historical or contemporary personality, describing some of the person's better-known decisions. Tell the students as much as you can about what went into making the decisions. *Or,* provide the students with details and clues concerning each decision and ask them to guess what it was. Discuss the importance of specific decisions from throughout history and how those decisions affect people today.

Tell the students you would like them to select a living or historical person who interests them, and research that person's life to find out about at least one key decision he or she made that affected the lives of many other people. Ask the students to see if they can determine whether the decision was the result of careful study, or intuition, or both. Suggest that they not overlook the possibility that the decision was irresponsible, impulsive, irrational, or the result of a premeditated plan to satisfy selfish motives.

Note: If you are studying a particular historical period or country, delimit the assignment accordingly.

Give the students several days to research and write their reports.

Discussion questions:

Ask the students to share their findings with one another in triads or small groups. Suggest that they follow circle session rules and procedures. After the small-group sessions, conduct a class discussion by asking the following questions:

1. Which decisions were made as the result of careful study, and which ones seemed to be based on intuition? Were any based on both?
2. How do some of these decisions affect us today?
3. Did most of these people realize at the time how important their decisions were to the lives of other people?
4. Which decisions do you admire and respect?
5. Which decisions seemed wrong, foolish, or irresponsible?
6. Which decisions do you think were the toughest ones to make?
7. If these people had to make the same decisions in today's world, what do you think they would do?

I Used Good Judgment
A Circle Session

Objectives:

The students will:

—describe a decision they made.

—define *judgment* and its role in decision-making.

Introduce the Topic:

In your own words, say to the students: *Our topic for this session is, "I Used Good Judgment." The point of this session is to discuss times when we used our judgment to make choices that worked out well for us. No one exercises perfect judgment all the time, but you and I have used good judgment on many occasions. Think of an example. Perhaps you used good judgment in the way you spent some money, or handled a problem, or asked for help in making a difficult decision. Maybe you thought over your decision very carefully, or perhaps you just knew what to do. Regardless of how long it took, or the exact process you used, the results verified that your judgment was sound. If you'd like to tell us about a time when you believe you exercised good judgment, we'd like to hear about it. The topic is, "I Used Good Judgment."*

Discussion questions:

1. How did you feel before you decided what to do?
2. How did you feel after you decided?
3. What constitutes good judgment?
4. If a decision doesn't work out the way you thought it would, does that mean you used bad judgment? Why or why not?
5. How can a good decision for one person be a bad decision for another?

Looking Back on a Decision I Made
A Circle Session

Objective:
The students will describe and evaluate decisions they have made.

Introduce the Topic:
Say to the students: *Our topic for this session is, "Looking Back on a Decision I Made." It's usually very easy for us to look back on something and see how we could have done it differently. That's called hindsight. Perhaps you made a decision once that you wouldn't make again today, or maybe, looking back, you feel proud of yourself for making the decision. Whatever the decision was, and whether or not you think it was a good decision now, if you would like to tell us about it, we would like to hear your story. The topic is, "Looking Back on a Decision I Made."*

Discussion questions:
1. How did you feel about your decision when you made it? How do you feel about it now?
2. Which decisions were made after gathering facts and thinking things over?
3. Which decisions were the result of intuition, hunches, or just "knowing?"
4. Did you learn anything in this session that will be useful to you when you make decisions from now on? If so, what?

Additional Circle Session Topics

A Time I Had to Choose the Best of Two Bad Things
I Had a Problem and Solved It
I Didn't Want to Have to Make a Decision
I Thought Over My Decision, and I Stuck to It
A Time I Shared in Making a Decision
A Time I Used Good Judgment
I Thought It Over and Then Decided
A Time I Had Trouble Deciding the Right Thing to Do
I Had to Remake My Decision
What I Would Do If I Were an Adult
Something I Would Like to Achieve in the Next Three Years
Things I Can Do to Get Where I Want to Be
How I Earned Something and What I Did with It
I Put Off Making a Decision
A Decision I Lived to Regret
A Decision Someone Else Made That Affected Me
It Was My Decision, But Someone Else Made It
The Hardest Decision I've Ever Made
One of the Best Decisions I've Ever Made
I Made a Good Decision But Got a Poor Result
The Hardest Thing About Making Decisions Is...
The Easiest Thing About Making Decisions Is...
What It Takes to Be Decisive
A Time I Was Sure I Was Doing the Right Thing
I Time I Decided Based on My Feelings
A Time Someone Made an Unfair Decision
I Made a Decision and Regretted It Later

Managing Stress

Activities in this unit teach students to:

- identify sources and effects of stress in their own lives.

- learn and practice two deep breathing exercises.

- describe specific ways to effectively manage stress.

Circle Sessions in this unit allow students to:

- identify situations that cause them stress and discuss coping behaviors.

- describe specific things they do to take care of their bodies and emotions.

You and Stress
Presentation, Experience Sheet, and Discussion

Objectives:

The students will:

—define stress and identify its three major sources.

—identify sources and effects of stress in their own life.

—explain how stress can lead to illness and reduced performance in all areas.

—describe how individual reactions and attitudes affect stress.

Materials:

the experience sheet, "The Juggling Act," an enlarged drawing of the juggler on chalkboard, chart paper, or overhead

Procedure:

Provide each student a copy of the experience sheet, "The Juggling Act." Go over the directions. Then, in your own words, make these comments: *Handling stress is a lot like a juggling act. The more balls, or stressors, you are trying to "keep in the air," the harder it is to stay in control. Pretend the balls are your stressors. Label them with the stressful situations, events, or problems that you've been juggling lately. Remember that exciting, positive events can be stressful, too. Inside the body of the juggler, locate areas where you are experiencing physical symptoms and write them down. For example, you might write the word "ache" inside the head of the juggler, or give the juggler a heart and write the word "pounding" next to it. List other symptoms, like jittery nerves, stomachache, colds, flu, and forgetfulness. Around the outside of the juggler, write down the external effects these stressors are having on your life. Falling grades, broken relationships, missed appointments, alcohol or other drug use, reduced leisure time, and lowered job performance are examples of external effects.*

Using your enlarged drawing of the juggler (on chalkboard, chart paper, or overhead), develop a composite of the student responses. Survey the students to elicit several different examples of stressors. Categorize them (e.g., personal relationships, parents, schoolwork, future) and write the categories on balls above your juggler's head. Draw symbols to represent body organs inside your juggler, survey the students for physical symptoms, and categorize and record these. Finally, survey the students for examples of external effects and list several categories of these around the outside of your chart.

Refer back to your composite at appropriate points and involve the students in discussion as you make these points about stress:

- Different people are stressed by different things. How people handle stress is also highly individual.
- Not all stress is bad. Happy circumstances, like winning the lottery, planning a surprise party, and meeting a new friend can be stressful, too.
- Much of the stress we experience comes from three sources: the environment (pollution, traffic, etc.), our body (injuries, illness, sleep disturbances, growth changes, etc.), and our thoughts (attitudes, fear, worry, etc.).
- Stress causes a "fight or flight" response within the body. Adrenaline is released into the blood stream, speeding up all of the body's systems.
- If the fight or flight response is prolonged, the body's immune system is depressed, and illness can result.
- Moderate stress can lead to better performance by providing you with extra energy.
- Each of us makes the determination whether or not to label an experience threatening. Maintaining a positive attitude and feeling in control of your life put you in a much better position to handle stress.

Discussion Questions:

1. How does your attitude affect your body's reaction to stress?
2. How can reinterpreting an event reduce the stress associated with it?
3. Can you think of a time when you consciously changed your attitude or reinterpreted an event to feel better?
4. How are stress and health connected?

The Juggling Act
Experience Sheet

How much stress are you trying to juggle? Here's a way to find out:
1. Next to the objects which the juggler is keeping in the air, list all the **stressful situations, events, or problems** that *you've* been dealing with lately. Include positive as well as negative.
2. Near the juggler's body, write down all the **physical symptoms** that you experience in *your* body as a result of the stressors you are juggling.
3. In the space around the juggler, write down the **external effects** these stressors are having on your life.

The Breath of Life
Two Breathing Exercises

Objectives:
The students will:
—learn and practice two deep breathing exercises.
—identify times when they can use breathing exercises for relaxation and renewal.

Materials:
chalkboard and chalk

Procedure:
Begin by telling the students that various breathing exercises have proven effective in reducing anxiety, irritability, muscular tension, fatigue, and depression. Point out that a simple but effective method of relaxation is the practice of deep breathing.

On the chalkboard, write the terms *thoracic breathing* and *diaphragmatic breathing*. Explain that thoracic breathing is shallow and takes place primarily in the upper part of the lungs, whereas diaphragmatic breathing is deep and emanates from the diaphragm. In your own words, explain: *The diaphragm is a muscle that separates the chest from the abdomen. When we breathe, the diaphragm expands and contracts. This action, though usually automatic, is subject to voluntary control. When air is inhaled, the diaphragm expands and tenses; when it is exhaled, the diaphragm relaxes. By lengthening the time we spend exhaling, we encourage full use of our lung capacity.*

To practice diaphragmatic breathing, have the students expand their abdomen so their stomach rises and falls with each breath while their chest size remains relatively constant. Explain that this action, which will probably feel forced and unnatural at first, provides sufficient oxygen to properly oxygenate the blood and maintain good mental and physical health.

Lead the students in two breathing exercises that are brief, easy, and well suited for the classroom. For the first exercise, the students may stand or sit in chairs. Have them stand away from their chairs or desks for the second exercise. Read the following directions aloud, pausing for a few seconds between steps. Lead a brief follow-up discussion.

The Deep-Breathing Exercise
1. *Sit up straight or stand erect, but relaxed.*
2. *Notice how you are breathing. Breathe slowly and deeply.*
3. *Close your eyes and breathe slowly through your nose. Inhale deeply so that the air fills the lower section of your lungs and your diaphragm pushes your stomach outward to make room for the air. Then, as your lower ribs and chest expand, fill the middle part of your lungs. Finally, as your chest rises slightly, fill the upper part of the lungs. Do this in one continuous motion as you inhale.*

4. *Hold the breath for a few seconds.*
5. *Exhale slowly through your nose and mouth. As you exhale, allow all of the tensions to leave your body.*
6. *Continue to breathe deeply like this until I tell you to stop (3 to 5 minutes).*
7. *Gently open your eyes. Stay seated (or standing) in the same position for a few moments.*

The Windmill-Breathing Exercise

1. *Stand straight with your arms extended in front of you.*
2. *Inhale deeply so that the air fills the lower section of your lungs and your diaphragm pushes your stomach outward to make room for the air. Then, as your lower ribs and chest expand, fill the middle part of your lungs. Finally, as your chest rises slightly, fill the upper part of the lungs. Do this in one continuous motion as you inhale.*
3. *Rotate your arms backward in a circle several times.*
4. *Reverse direction and rotate your arms forward, or alternate directions like a windmill.*
5. *Exhale forcefully through your mouth.*
6. *Breathe several deep, purifying breaths.*

Discussion questions:

1. How did you feel while doing these exercises? How did you feel after you were finished?
2. Have you ever used deep breathing to help you relax? How did it work?
3. How can we use these short exercises to relieve stress here in class? How will you use them outside of school?

Relax and Enjoy Life
Discussion and Experience Sheet

Objectives:
The students will:
—describe ways to avoid the harmful effects of stress.
—identify specific ways to manage stress effectively.
—discuss how unmanaged stress can be harmful.

Materials:
pens or pencils, one copy of the experience sheet, "Relax a Little" for each student, and chalkboard or easel with chart paper

Procedure:
Introduce the activity by saying to the students: *One of the things that people enjoy most is relaxation. Relaxation can involve many aspects, and there are many different ways to relax. Some people relax by doing something athletic like running or engaging in a sport. Other people relax by resting or reading. Still others relax by listening to music they enjoy or being with friends.*

After drawing the attention of the students to the ways people relax, ask them to share some examples of their own. As they do so, write down their comments on the board or chart paper under the heading, "Ways We Relax." Suggest that the students jot down any new ideas they get from the list concerning good ways to relax.

After creating the list, ask the students to think about *why* people relax. Make a list of their comments on the board or chart paper under the heading, "Why We Relax." Help them along by suggesting reasons of your own, particularly reasons connected with some of the feelings that relaxation generates.

Now compare the two lists and point out that by doing the things described on the first list they can generate the feelings described on the second list.

Distribute the "Relax a Little" experience sheet. Ask the students to think about the things they do—or would like to do—to relax. Have them note these on their experience sheets. Next to each item they list, ask the students to write down how they feel when they participate in that activity. Finally, have the students write down three things that cause them to feel stress and, next to each, record how the stress makes them feel.

Conclusion:
After the students have completed their experience sheets, emphasize that by taking the time to do something relaxing when they are experiencing stress, the students can substitute good feelings for bad.

Extension:
Encourage the students to start relaxing as a way of effectively managing stress. Point out that developing the habit of relaxing regularly can take a lot of practice. Put a sign up in the room that says, "Feel Good Today—Relax A Little." Each day for two weeks, take a moment to remind students to relax when they experience stress. After two weeks have passed, conduct a circle session using the topic, "A Way I Relaxed to Reduce Stress."

Relax A Little
Experience Sheet

Ways that I can relax:

_____
_____
_____
_____
_____
_____
_____

How I feel when I'm relaxing:

_____
_____
_____
_____
_____
_____
_____
_____
_____

Three things that happen in my life that cause me to feel stress:

1. _____
_____
2. _____
_____
3. _____
_____

How this stress makes me feel:

_____
_____
_____
_____
_____

Because stress causes us to feel badly in many different ways, a very good approach to feeling better right away is to do something that is relaxing. Substitute the good feelings of relaxing for the bad feelings of stress!

What I Do When The Going Gets Tough
A Circle Session

Objectives:

The students will:

—identify stressful experiences.

—describe positive ways of handling stress.

Introduce the Topic:

Say to the students: *Our topic for this session is, "What I Do When the Going Gets Tough." Most of us have ways to make ourselves feel better when we are stressed. What's one of your ways? What do you do to help yourself when you feel angry, worried, tense, or nervous? Maybe you talk to one of your parents or to a friend about what's bothering you. Or perhaps you take a long walk or bike ride. Spending time alone with your pet may make you feel better. Or perhaps you do something to take your mind off the stressful situation—like watching TV, going to a movie, or reading a book. Tell us what you do, and how you feel when you do it. Let's think it over for a few moments. The topic is, "What I Do When the Going Gets Tough."*

Discussion questions:

1. Why is it important to find positive ways to handle stress?
2. What are some negative ways in which people try to handle stress?
3. Do you think fewer people would use alcohol and drugs if they knew how to handle stress in more positive ways?

Something That Causes Me Stress
A Circle Session

Objectives:
The students will:
—describe causes of personal stress.
—discuss specific things that can be done to relieve stress.
—state that feelings of stress are normal.

Introduce the Topic:
Our topic for this session is, "Something That Causes Me Stress." Do you ever get tongue tied? Feel uptight or on edge? Get a headache or a queezie stomach when you're not sick? Chances are the cause of those feelings is stress. Many different things can cause stress—worrying about a test, feeling angry at someone, or not getting enough sleep, for example. Even good things can cause stress—like the excitement of waiting for a special event. Think of something that causes you stress and tell us how you handle it. What happens to cause the stress, and how does it affect the way you feel, the thoughts you have, and the things you do? Take a few minutes to think about it. The topic is, "Something That Causes Me Stress."

Discussion questions:
1. Why do people experience stress?
2. Do the same kinds of things frequently cause you stress?
3. If you know something is likely to stress you, what can you do about it in advance?
4. When you feel stressed, what can you do to relieve the symptoms?

Additional Circle Session Topics
I Was So Distressed I Got Sick
I Did Something for My Body and It Improved My Spirit
Something I Worried About That Turned Out Okay
I Problem I'm Trying to Solve
Someone I Can Talk to When I'm Worried
My Favorite Physical Exercise
Where I Go When I Want to Be Alone
A Way I Take Care of My Body
What I Say When I Talk to Myself
A Way I've Learned to Calm Myself Down
Music That Makes Me Feel Good
A Time I Felt Upset and Didn't Know Why
Something I Do for My Own Well Being
A Time I Felt A Lot of Tension and Stress

Self-Concept

Activities in this unit teach students to:

- describe specific qualities and characteristics which they possess.

- identify strengths, talents, and special abilities about themselves.

- distinguish between how others see them and how they see themselves, and between present self-concept and desired self-concept.

Circle Sessions in this unit allow students to:

- explain how the recognition of personal attributes contributes to self-esteem.

- describe specific areas of personal growth.

How We See Ourselves
Self-Assessment, Sharing, and Discussion

Objectives:

Group members will:

—rate the degree to which they possess specific qualities/characteristics.

—represent their self-concept pictorially or in words.

—describe how self-concept affects daily living.

Materials:

one copy of the experience sheet, "Looking At Me" for each student; fine- and medium-point colored markers for students who choose to draw an image of themselves

Procedure:

Begin with a brief discussion about self-concept. Remind the students that self-concept is like looking in the mirror, except that the image we have depends more on our thoughts and conclusions about ourselves than it does on the physical mechanisms involved in sight. Point out that people often see themselves quite differently than others see them.

Distribute the experience sheets and briefly review the directions. Give the students about 15 minutes to complete the sheet. Make colored marking pens available to students who wish to draw pictures of themselves instead of writing paragraphs.

If the group is large, have the students form smaller groupings (three to five) and share their self-assessments and drawings/paragraphs. If the group is small, complete this part of the activity as a total group. Emphasize that all sharing is voluntary, and that students may keep any or all parts of the experience sheet confidential if they choose.

Conclude the activity by facilitating further discussion about self-concept.

Discussion questions:

1. Did you learn anything about yourself from this activity that surprised you? What was it?
2. What strengths did your self-assessment reveal?
3. What qualities would you like to develop more of?
4. What qualities would you like to reduce or eliminate?
5. What qualities or concerns did you discover you have in common with other members of the group?
6. How does self-concept affect our performance at school? ...our relations with other people? ...our outlook on life and the future?

Looking At Me
Self-Assessment

Read through the list of characteristics, below. Decide how well each characteristic fits YOU. Be honest. If you are unsure about an item, ask yourself how others see you. Circle the point on the scale that describes you best.

	Most of the time		Average		Almost never
1. Well-liked	●	●	●	●	●
2. Good looking	●	●	●	●	●
3. Intelligent	●	●	●	●	●
4. Popular	●	●	●	●	●
5. Athletic	●	●	●	●	●
6. Appreciated	●	●	●	●	●
7. Talented	●	●	●	●	●
8. Happy	●	●	●	●	●
9. Worried	●	●	●	●	●
10. Relaxed	●	●	●	●	●
11. Caring	●	●	●	●	●
12. Strong	●	●	●	●	●
13. Unique	●	●	●	●	●
14. Assertive	●	●	●	●	●
15. Enthusiastic	●	●	●	●	●
16. Energetic	●	●	●	●	●
17. Tense	●	●	●	●	●
18. Dependable	●	●	●	●	●
19. A good friend	●	●	●	●	●
20. Boring	●	●	●	●	●
21. Tough	●	●	●	●	●
22. Confident	●	●	●	●	●
23. Unhappy	●	●	●	●	●
24. Creative	●	●	●	●	●
25. A leader	●	●	●	●	●
26. Friendly	●	●	●	●	●
27. Helpful	●	●	●	●	●
28. Responsible	●	●	●	●	●
29. Fun	●	●	●	●	●
30. Angry	●	●	●	●	●
31. Honest	●	●	●	●	●
32. Successful	●	●	●	●	●
33. A loner	●	●	●	●	●
34. Shy	●	●	●	●	●
35. Generous	●	●	●	●	●

On the other side of this paper, draw a picture or write a paragraph that describes your thoughts and feelings about yourself.

A Feeling of Accomplishment
Oral Presentation and Discussion

Objectives:

The students will:

—identify strengths, talents, and special abilities in self and others.

—practice methods of positive self-talk.

—describe how positive self-talk enhances self-esteem.

Procedure:

Introduce the activity by saying to the students: *One of the most powerful motivators for doing something is anticipating the feeling of accomplishment that we experience when the task is finished.*

Announce that you want the students to take a mental inventory of their activities and identify one that they can always depend on to give them a sense of pride and achievement. Explain that their assignment has two parts. First, they are to prepare a brief oral presentation (3 to 5 minutes) explaining the activity they take pride in. Second, they are to bring something to class on the day of their presentation that somehow illustrates or demonstrates what they are talking about. Elaborate:

Perhaps you get enjoyment out of working with computers and can bring in a piece of software you use regularly or something that you've produced using a computer. Maybe you enjoy drawing because every completed picture is a proud new creation. If so, bring a drawing for us to see. If cooking gives you feelings of accomplishment, bring in your favorite recipe, or better yet some samples. If

you like science, show us an experiment you've completed, or a science book you enjoy. Your presentation doesn't have to be extensive; we're interested in whatever you tell us.

Allow a few students a day to give their presentations and show or demonstrate the item they brought. Give every presenter your undivided attention and plenty of appreciation and recognition. On the last day of the presentations, conclude the activity with a general discussion.

Discussion questions

1. Why is it important to accomplish things?
2. What do accomplishments have to do with self-esteem?
3. What are some examples of small, everyday accomplishments?
4. How can you use self-talk to remind yourself of your accomplishments?

Four Concepts
Creative Self-Assessment and Discussion

Objectives:
Group members will:
—distinguish between how others see them and how they see themselves.
—distinguish between present self-concept and desired self-concept.

Materials:
one copy of the experience sheet, "Concepts of Me" for each student; fine- and medium-tip marking pens in various colors

Procedure:
Remind the students of the definition of self-concept. (You may wish to distinguish between self-*concept* and self-*esteem*. Self-concept is one's <u>view</u> of self; self-esteem is the <u>value</u> placed on that view.)

Distribute the experience sheets, and place the marking pens where the students can share them. Go over the directions printed on the sheet. Emphasize that the students may employ descriptive word lists, paragraph descriptions, illustrations, symbols — even poetry — to complete their four descriptions. Suggest they begin with quadrant 1, and do the rest in any sequence they wish.

Allow sufficient time for thinking and creativity. When the students have finished, have them read (or show) and explain their descriptions to the group. Facilitate discussion.

Discussion questions:
1. Why do others see us differently than we see ourselves?
2. If you asked your best friend to describe you, which quadrant would his/her description match most closely? Why?
3. Which quadrants do you wish were more similar?
4. What can you do to bring those images closer together?

Concepts of Me
Experience Sheet

Your *self-concept* is how you *view* yourself. It is what you *think about* yourself. Other people also have a concept of you. In the spaces below, write or draw four descriptions (concepts) of you. Notice their similarities and differences.

1. The concept I have of myself:	**3. The concept I would like to have of myself:**
2. The concept others have of me:	**4. The concept I would like others to have of me:**

Success Bombardment
Experience Sheet and Group Exercise

Objectives:

The students will:

—recognize and describe their own worth and worthiness.

—identify strengths, talents, and special abilities in themselves and others.

—practice positive self-talk.

Note: For optimum impact, use this activity after your students have had time to develop as a group, e.g., have experienced several activities together.

Materials:

one copy of the experience sheet, "Success Inventory," for each student; 12 small self-adhesive labels per student; and 1 copy of the "Target" worksheet for each student

Procedure:

Distribute the experience sheet. Go over the directions and answer any questions. Have the students work individually to fill out the sheets. Allow about 15 minutes. If the students appear to be having trouble thinking of accomplishments, take a couple of minutes and talk to the entire class about such examples as learning to: *walk, talk, dress, dance, play, sing, count, problem-solve, read, write, love; ride a bike, skateboard, roller-skate; ski, play softball, volleyball, soccer, basketball; cook, play an instrument, use a computer, be a friend, join an organization; earn a merit badge, award, or certificate; learn to type, baby-sit, drive a car, care for a pet; etc., etc.*

When the students have completed their sheets, ask them to form groups of four or five. Give 12 small, blank, self-adhesive labels and a "Target" worksheet to each student.

Direct the students to take turns describing their accomplishments to the other members of their group. In your own words, explain: *Tell your group why you picked those particular successes. Explain how you felt about them at the time they occurred and why they are particularly meaningful to you now. Immediately after you share, the other members of your group will each make three labels that describe positive things about you based on the successes you shared. For example, the first person's labels might say, "industrious and energetic," "musically talented," and "born to lead." Then, while you hold up your "target," that person will look directly at you, tell you what he or she has written on each label, and stick the labels on your target. The other members of your group will then take a turn "bombarding" you with their success labels in the same manner. If there are three other people in your group (total of four), you will end up with nine labels on your target. A second person in the group will then take a turn reading his or her successes and being "bombarded." Then a third person will be the target, and so on.*

Circulate and assist the groups, as needed. Although the students are expected to enjoy the exercise, make sure that they appreciate its seriousness and do not engage in any kind of teasing or put-downs. If you observe any student using the third person ("She is industrious and energetic.") when labeling a "target," stop the person and help him or her rephrase the statement in the second person. ("You are industrious and energetic.") Lead a follow-up discussion.

Discussion Questions:

1. How do you feel after doing this exercise?
2. What did you learn about yourself? ...about other members of your group?
3. How did you decide which accomplishments to include on your list?
4. Why do you suppose we spend so much time thinking about our failures and deficiencies when we have all accomplished so much?
5. Where can you put your target so that it will continue to remind you of your successes?

Success Inventory
Experience Sheet

Your life is a chronicle of successes, one after another, year after year. The things you've accomplished could fill a book. Look back now at the child you were and the young adult you have become. Recall some of the many things you've learned and achieved, and write the most memorable here:

- **Five skills I mastered before the age of 5 were:**

1. _____

2. _____

3. _____

4. _____

5. _____

- **Four things I accomplished between the ages of 5 and 8 were:**

1. _____

2. _____

3. _____

4. _____

- **Four of my achievements between the ages of 8 and 11 were:**

1. _____

2. _____

3. _____

4. _____

• **Three major things I accomplished between the ages of 11 and 13 were:**

1. _____

2. _____

3. _____

• **Three of my successes between the ages of 13 and now are:**

1. _____

2. _____

3. _____

Target Worksheet

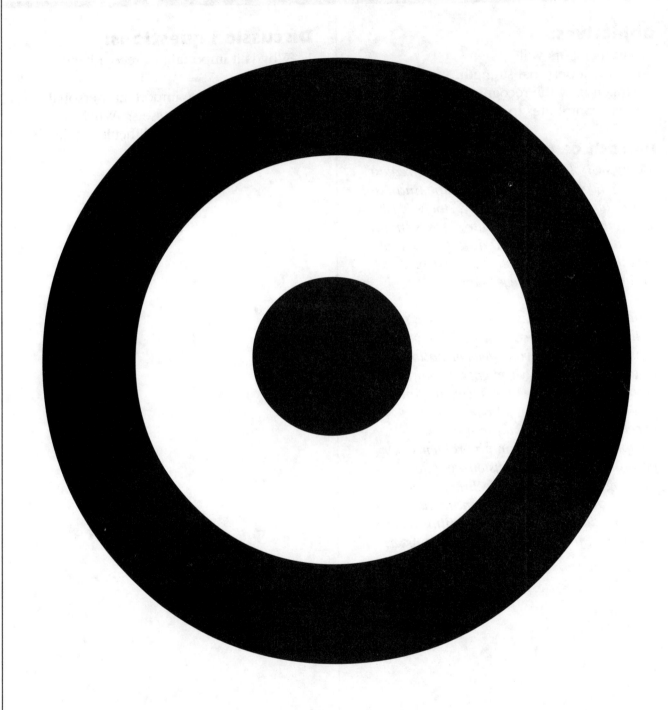

My Greatest Asset
A Circle Session

Objectives:

Group members will:
—identify a personal strength.
—explain how the recognition of personal assets contributes to self-esteem.

Introduce the Topic:

Today's Circle Session topic is, "My Greatest Asset." Everyone has assets. In the financial world, our assets are property, stocks, cash — things that add to our wealth. Assets in our personal lives represent a different kind of wealth. They are the attributes we possess and the skills we've developed.

What is your greatest asset? Maybe it's your ability to speak a second language, your sense of humor, or your determination even in tough situations. It might be your loyalty, your ability to make others feel comfortable, or your sense of style. Maybe you are excellent at drawing, dancing, writing, computing, or solving math problems. Or perhaps you're good at listening, often hearing what others are feeling but not saying. Review some of the many assets you have, and choose the one you think is your greatest. Our topic is, "My Greatest Asset."

Discussion questions:

1. Why is it important to recognize our assets?
2. Which are more important, personal assets or financial assets? Why?
3. Why is it sometimes difficult to talk about ourselves positively?

Self-Understanding I've Recently Gained
A Circle Session

Objectives:

The students will:

—verbalize the importance of self-awareness and understanding.

—describe specific areas of personal growth.

Introduce the Topic:

Say to the students: *Today we're going to talk about things we've learned about ourselves recently. Our topic is, "Self-Understanding I've Recently Gained."*

By self-understanding, we mean learning something about yourself that you didn't know before—such as why you do things a certain way, or why you react to people or situations the way you do. Maybe you recently figured out why you feel fear or happiness or excitement at certain times. Or perhaps you've had a major breakthrough in understanding why you act the way you do around certain people. Possibly you decided recently what kind of career would be best for you, or what talents you value most in yourself and want to develop. So take a moment to think about this. The topic is, "Self-Understanding I've Recently Gained."

Discussion questions:

1. What similarities and differences did you notice in the kinds of things we've recently learned about ourselves?
2. How did you arrive at your self-understanding?
3. What value is there in understanding yourself better?

Additional Circle Session Topics

What People Like About Me

Something I'm Good At

I Did Something That Made Me Feel Like a Good Person

Something I Did or Made That I'm Proud Of

Something I Accomplished That Really Pleased Me

A Time I Made a Big Effort and Succeeded

A Time I Knew I Could Do It

Something About Me That's Special

Something I Like About Myself

Something I Wish I Could Do Better

A Success I Recently Experienced

A Time I Won and Loved It

A Time I Lost and Took It Hard

First I Imagined It, Then I Created It

When Someone Expected the Very Best of Me

Personal Responsibility

Activities in this unit teach students to:

- develop and describe rules of conduct for living in a fictional society.

- define responsible behavior.

- discuss the benefits and challenges of responsible, ethical behavior.

Circle Sessions in this unit allow students to:

- describe incidents in which they behaved responsibly.

- identify ways in which they can contribute to the betterment of the community/world.

The Rules I'd Like to Live By
Creative Thinking, Writing and Discussion

Objectives:

The students will:

—develop and describe rules of conduct for living in a fictional society.

—discuss positive and negative considerations of having governments.

Materials:

writing materials

Procedure:

Divide the class into an even number of small groups, not exceeding six members each. Explain that each group has been stranded on a desert island with no hope of rescue. Food is plentiful and there is unlimited drinking water. Their task is to draw up a list of rules to be followed in the following areas:

    A. What will be considered basic human rights?

    B. How will decisions be reached?

    C. What if someone dissents?

    D. How will justice and injustice be determined?

    E. How will property be divided?

    F. How will work be allocated?

    G. Who will educate the children and how?

Tell the students that they should select someone to write down the rules that the group agrees upon. Tell the students they will have the rest of the period and all of the next one to develop their rules. Then let them begin.

Conclusion:

In the next class session, ask the groups to share their rules with one other group. Ask the students in the combined groups to sit in a large circle and select a leader to conduct the sharing session. The leader's job is to make sure that only one person speaks at a time. Tell the students that the session will last approximately 30 minutes. Urge them to divide the time equally between the two groups, and signal them at the halfway point.

Extension:

In a fourth class period, have a guest speaker talk to the students. Choose a person who has lived in a community, such as Synanon, a kibbutz, a religious community, a commune, etc. Ask the speaker to describe the community's rules and how they were established, and to tell the students about the values of the community, which the rules were designed to support.

Note: This activity is very effective when used as an introduction to a history unit focusing on the Constitution of the United States (or another republic).

Freedom and Responsibility
A Class Reaction Session and Discussion

Objectives:
The students will:
—define what is responsible behavior in three situations.
—discuss the meaning of freedom and its relationship to responsibility.

Materials:
writing materials

Procedure:
Read the following quotation to the class and discuss its meaning:

Freedom is a partial, negative aspect of responsibility which is richer and more complete in meaning. We may become free from the immediate and yet remain irresponsible. We cannot become responsible, however, without also becoming free.

> John Wild
> *Existence and the World of Freedom*

Tell the students you are going to read them several brief stories. Explain that each story is followed by some thinking questions. Ask them to listen to each one very carefully and, after you've read the story and its accompanying questions, write some brief notes to themselves about how they see the situation. Their notes should relate to:

1. Who is responsible to whom.
2. What the individuals should do in order to behave responsibly.
3. Any specific question asked.

The Stories:

Judy and the Orioles
The Orioles girls' softball team has been practicing after school at the park and winning most of its Saturday games. Judy is the best pitcher. The most important game of the season is coming up next weekend, a three-day holiday. It will determine which teams make the finals. Everything is going fine until Judy tells the girls on her team that for months her parents have been planning a camping trip for that weekend, and they expect her to go with them. The members of the team become angry and upset. They try to convince Judy to stay and pitch, but she says she's free to do as she pleases.
- *Who is responsible for what? ...to whom?*
- *Is Judy responsible to the team, to her parents, or to herself?*
- *Are Judy's parents responsible to the team?*
- *Is it the coach's responsibility to persuade Judy's parents to cancel the trip or allow Judy to stay?*
- *Was it Judy's responsibility to check the schedule and see that her parents were informed?*
- *How much freedom should Judy have in this situation to decide what to do?*

Tony's Father Quits
Tony's father has been a responsible worker on the same job for 15 years. Because of this, Tony has had the typical advantages of an upper-middle-class student—clothes,

money, and just about any other reasonable thing he needs or wants. Then one day Tony's father suddenly announces that he hates what he's doing for a living. He says he can't take another day of it, quits his job, and goes on unemployment.

For years Tony has assumed that his father would buy him a new car for his 16th birthday and send him to Hawaii for the summer, but neither of those things will be possible now. In fact, his father tells him there will be no more allowances, and if he wants money for anything other than basic things like food, he will have to work for it himself. Tony protests. He insists that his father owes him an allowance, the car, and the trip. He says he assumed these were his rights all along. He also tells his father he has no right to quit his job without checking with the rest of the family first. Tony's father says Tony is confused. He tells Tony he is free to do what he wants.

- *What basic responsibilities does Tony's father have to Tony and the rest of the family?*
- *Does he really have the freedom or the right to quit his job?*
- *Is he responsible to Tony to give him an allowance, buy him a car, or send him to Hawaii?*
- *What are his (the father's) responsibilities to himself?*
- *Is Tony responsible as a family member to be kind and understanding during a difficult time in his father's life?*

Krontz Faces Pollution Charges
Samuel Krontz owns a factory. Years ago his factory made large profits, but he and the board of directors invested the money unwisely and lost almost all of it. Now the business has a lot of competition; costs of production and salaries for workers are

rising. The corporation is barely able to stay alive. Besides that, the factory is old, and there is not enough money in the corporation to tear it down and build a new one. The possibilities of getting a large enough loan to do the job are very slim because of the corporation's bad deals in the past. Despite all these troubles the factory does provide employment to 2,000 workers.

Several years ago, Mr. Krontz started getting a lot of complaints about the smoke pouring out of the factory's smokestacks. Combined with the smoke from other factories in the area, the smog is so bad that on some days people can't see further than a block in the city. The smog is causing their eyes to burn, and it's being blamed for the deaths of many people in the city with respiratory problems. Since those first complaints, more and more people have become upset about the pollution. Mr. Krontz doesn't know what to do. He's sure there's no way he can build a new, modern factory that wouldn't put out so much smoke. If he shuts the factory down, 2,000 people will be out of work.

- *Should Mr. Krontz be free to do whatever he wants?*
- *To whom is Mr. Krontz responsible, the people in the city and neighboring cities, the 2,000 workers and their families, or the corporation's board of directors and stockholders?*
- *What would be the most responsible thing for him to do?*
- *Should he try to get a loan to rebuild the factory, even though he's sure he won't get enough?*
- *Should he close the factory?*
- *Should he keep things as they are?*
- *Should he seek other solutions?*

Ask the students to form triads and share their reactions to the stories.

Suggest that they select one story to discuss in depth, rather than attempting to discuss all three in a cursory manner. Remind the students to follow circle session rules and procedures, and not to expect total agreement. Their goal is to allow each triad member enough time, without interruptions, to explain who he or she sees as being responsible to whom, and what constitutes responsible behavior in each situation. Allow about 15 minutes for triad interaction.

Discussion questions:

Engage the whole class in a culminating discussion. Some suggested questions are:

1. What did you agree on in your triad?
2. What differences of opinion did you have?
3. Why is it important for people to understand to whom they are responsible?
4. When do we have a right to be responsible to ourselves?
5. What makes behavior responsible or irresponsible?
6. Did anyone in any of these stories misunderstand the meaning of freedom?

Extension:

Instead of reading the stories to the class, work with a group of students to create and rehearse three short skits that dramatize the stories. Have the group present their skits to the class, and carry out the rest of the activity as suggested.

The Way I See It
Research, Writing, Reports, and Discussion

Objectives:

The students will:

—define responsible and irresponsible behavior in specific situations.

—define ethical and unethical behavior in specific situations.

—discuss the benefits and challenges of responsible, ethical behavior.

Materials:

a biography of a famous (or infamous) individual who lived in the past, and a current newspaper or news magazine; writing materials

Procedure:

Bring the biography and newspaper or news magazine with you to class. Tell the class in your own words about the person described in the biography, emphasizing his/her behaviors. Then open the newspaper or news magazine and summarize an article that concerns the conduct of individuals and/ or nations. In neither of these presentations label anything "responsible," "irresponsible," "ethical," or "unethical." Rather, describe fully what the people and/or nations did, allowing the students to reach their own conclusions.

Next, ask the class: *Did anything I've been describing from either the biography or the newspaper or news magazine strike you as being ethical or unethical—responsible or irresponsible? If so, what?*

Allow as many students as wish to respond the opportunity to do so. Briefly add your own opinions as you see fit.

Explain to the class that their assignment is to choose one of the following three options and write a report of at least 100 words:

1. Using a biography, investigate the actions of a famous or infamous person from the past.
2. Using a current newspaper or news magazine, learn about what an individual or nation has recently done.
3. Interview an adult in a responsible position to learn about his/her duties. (Any position in which a person is in charge of what happens to other people is a responsible position.)

In each case, the report should constitute the opinion of the writer. The students should explain what behaviors they see as responsible and irresponsible, ethical or unethical, that the person (or nation) has done or routinely does. Remind the students to support their conclusions.

After the reports have been completed, ask the students to share their evaluations in small groups of four to six. Allow about 15 to 20 minutes. Lead a culminating class discussion.

Discussion questions:

1. What similarities did you notice in what most or all of us saw as responsible, ethical behaviors?
2. What kinds of things did most of us see as being irresponsible or unethical?
3. When is it easy to be responsible?
4. What rewards do you get for behaving ethically?
5. What boomerangs can occur with irresponsible or unethical behavior?
6. Does our nation reward unethical behavior, or at least look the other way? If so, what can be done about that?

A Situation in Which I Behaved Responsibly
A Circle Session

Objectives:

The students will:

—define responsible behavior.

—describe a situation in which they behaved responsibly.

—discuss the benefits of responsible behavior.

Introduce the Topic:

Say to the students: *Today in our circle session, we are going to take some deserved credit. The topic is, "A Situation in Which I Behaved Responsibly." Before we go any further, let's take a couple of minutes to talk about what responsible behavior is and why people think it's so great. Do you have any ideas?*

Listen to the students' comments. Then, in your own words, explain: *The word itself, response-able, says a lot. It means being **able** to respond, to do something you think is right, not just sit there and do nothing. In other words, when you take care of a situation and yourself, you've behaved responsibly. You can feel proud of yourself. It may have been simple, or it may have been hard, but you did it!*

Think that over. You can probably remember lots of times when you behaved responsibly. See if there isn't one you'd like to tell us about. If there is, we'd like to hear what happened, how you felt, and what you did. The topic is, "A Situation in Which I Behaved Responsibly."

Discussion questions:

1. How do you feel now about the responsible behavior you described?
2. What rewards do you get for responsible behavior?
3. What are some of the consequences of irresponsible behavior?
4. Did you hear any good ideas for ways to behave responsibly that you might not have thought of before?

Something I've Done (or Could Do) to Improve Our World
A Circle Session

Objective:

The students will describe ways in which they can contribute to the betterment of the community/world.

Introduce the Topic:

Say to the students: *The topic for this session is, "Something I've Done (or Could Do) to Improve Our World." Can you think of a time when you did something that you felt really helped, even in a small way, to improve the world we live in? Perhaps you improved a condition of some kind on your street or in your community. Maybe you helped change something that you thought was wrong. Or perhaps you did something to help the ecology—like making careful use of resources like water and electricity, or treating animals with care. Whatever it is, we would like to hear about it. If you can't think of something you've already done, perhaps you can think of something you would like to do in the future, either independently or with a group. Our topic is, "Something I've Done (or Could Do) to Improve Our World."*

Discussion questions:

1. How are feelings of apathy developed?
2. How can we create an atmosphere in this community/country that will encourage people to take action to improve things?
3. How do you feel when you do something that helps improve our world?

Additional Circle Sessions Topics

A Time I Kept My Promise
How I Help at School
How I Show That I'm a Good Citizen
How I Show Respect Toward Others
A Time I Helped Without Being Asked
A Promise That Was Hard to Keep
I Admitted That I Did It
I Faced a Problem on My Own
I Told the Truth and Was Glad
I Kept an Agreement
A Way in Which I'm Responsible
A Time I Did Something to Help the Community
What I Wish I Could Do to Make This a Better World
People Seem to Respect Me When...
Someone Tried to Make Me Do Something I Didn't Want to Do
I Do My Best in School When...
A Time I Said "No" to Peer Pressure
A Way I Changed to Be a Better Friend
A Rule We Have in My Family
I Said Yes When I Wanted to Say No
A Time I Had the Courage of My Convictions
My Favorite Excuse
A Responsibility I Have at Home
A Time Someone Made a Promise to Me and Kept It
A Time I Didn't Keep My Promise
I Took a Positive Attitude Toward One of My Responsibilities
A Task I Didn't Like at First, But Do Like Now
An Irresponsible Habit I've Decided to Drop
A Responsible Habit I Plan to Have as an Adult

Empathy

Activities in this unit teach students to:

- define the term *clique* and state how they can avoid making others feel left out.

- describe how a person might feel in response to being excluded.

- identify the negative effects of stereotyping labels.

Circle Sessions in this unit allow students to:

- describe an incident in which they were excluding.

- identify their reactions to acts of intolerance and prejudice.

The Clique Phenomenon
Brainstorming, Discussion, and Experience Sheet

Objectives:
The students will:
—identify ways to make new friends.
—define the term *clique* and describe the effects of cliques.
—state how they can avoid making other people feel left out.

Materials:
the experience sheet, "Getting On Your Own Side;" chalkboard or chart paper

Procedure:
Have the students form two teams. Give the teams 10 to 15 minutes to brainstorm a list describing as many ways as they can think of to make new friends. At the end of the allotted time, reconvene the class and ask the groups to share their lists. Possible ideas include:
• Sit beside someone different in the cafeteria and say hello.
• Offer to show someone new around the school.
• Join a school organization.
• Offer to help someone carry a heavy load.
• Team up with someone you don't know very well to work on a class project.
• Run an ad in the school paper asking for a companion for particular activities, like hiking or bicycling.
• Ask someone you know to introduce you to new people.
• Go to the gym or track after school and say hello to the kids who are practicing.

Write the word *clique* on the board and ask the students to help you define it. One possible definition might be:

An in-group or gang of kids that defines itself as much by who is excluded as by who is included.

Discuss how a clique's policy of exclusion causes members to have difficulty making new friends, and can completely frustrate the efforts of someone who is not in the clique to become good friends with someone who is. Stress that the reason many kids want to be a part of a clique is that they want to be liked by important" people and feel important themselves.

Ask the students to turn to the experience sheet, "Getting On Your Own Side." Allow the students about 10 minutes to complete the sheet. Then ask them to rejoin their teams and (voluntarily) share their answers to the questions.

Encourage the students to commit to making one new friend before the next session or to including one new person in their existing group of friends. Stipulate that before they can claim to have completed this assignment, the students must do something tangible with the new friend, such as sit together at an assembly, eat lunch together, go jogging or bicycling together, visit each other's home, see a movie together, or play video games after school. Ask the students to pay particular attention to the "Clique phenomenon" and avoid doing anything that causes another person to feel left out. Conclude the activity with a discussion.

Discussion questions:

1. In what ways do you think cliques are good?
2. In what ways do you think cliques are harmful?
3. Have you ever wanted to belong to a clique? If so, why was it important?
4. What would happen if there were no cliques at this school?
5. What kinds of cliques do adults have?

Getting on Your Own Side
Experience Sheet

Is it worth It to be In?

What have you done to be Included In a group?

I have . . .

___Yes ___No • risked losing friends.

___Yes ___No • hurt people who thought they were my friends by making them feel left out.

___Yes ___No • done something I thought was not right.

___Yes ___No • done something I knew was against the law.

___Yes ___No • drunk alcohol or used drugs.

___Yes ___No • done something that might have harmed me physically.

___Yes ___No • done something that cost me a lot of money.

___Yes ___No • done something that interfered with my school work.

___Yes ___No • done something my parents would have objected to if they had known.

___Yes ___No • done whatever was necessary, as long as it didn't harm anyone else.

___Yes ___No • done something that was against my religion.

___Yes ___No • done whatever was necessary.

Can you remember a time when you were pressured to exclude someone from an activity?

How did you feel? _____

_____

_____

_____

_____

_____

What did you do? _____

_____

_____

_____

_____

_____

If this ever happens again, what do you think

you will do? _____

_____

_____

_____

_____

_____

How It Feels To Be Left Out
Creative Writing and Discussion

Objectives:
The students will:
—describe in writing how a person might feel in response to being excluded.
—describe behavioral choices available in response to rejection/exclusion.

Materials:
writing materials

Procedure:
Explain to the students that you would like them to write about the topic, "How It Feels to Be Left Out." Emphasize that they will need to use their imaginations, because they are going to write from the viewpoint of a person of a different race or culture, or a person with a disability.

In your own words, explain to the students: *Imagine a situation in which a person might be excluded. Think about how you feel when you are left out of a group or activity that you really want to participate in. How might the situation and/or the feelings be the same or different for someone of a different race or culture, or someone with a disability? If the feelings would be about the same, what would they be? If the feelings would be different, how would they be different, and what would they be like? You might begin your story when the person is just starting to think about joining the group or activity. Describe what happens that leads to the rejection, and concentrate on the expression of feelings throughout.*

Ask the students to indicate at the end of their papers whether or not they would be willing to read their story to the class. Collect the papers and evaluate them in your usual manner, then return them to the students. Suggest that the students rewrite their papers as homework. At a subsequent class meeting, ask volunteers to read their stories to the class. Facilitate a discussion after each reading, basing your questions on issues presented in the story. Conclude the activity with a general discussion.

Discussion questions:
1. How are the feelings of most people the same in response to rejection? How are they different for people who belong to a minority race or culture? ...for people who have a disability?
2. What did you discover about your own attitudes towards people who belong to minorities or have disabilities?
3. What good does it do to try to understand each other's feelings?
4. What new ideas did you get about rejecting others? ...about handling rejection? ...about the idea of inclusion?

Pigeonholes and Stereotypes
Experiments with Labelling Language

Objectives:

The students will:

—identify specific labels used to stereotype individuals and groups.

—invent stereotyping labels for themselves and others in the group.

—describe the negative effects of stereotyping labels.

Materials:

chalkboard or chart paper

Procedure:

Talk to the students about the dehumanization caused by spoken and written language habits that either fail to promote individuality or associate people with stereotyping labels. Ask the students to help you brainstorm a list of stereotyping language. Write all ideas on the board. Include the following examples:

Groups of people are stereotyped by labels such as:

- The old
- Those foreigners
- The retarded
- The handicapped
- The homeless
- The blacks

Individuals are stereotyped by labels such as:

- A TMR (Trainable Mentally Retarded)
- An Illegal alien
- A welfare mother
- A Quad (Quadriplegic)

Many times, individuals or groups are referred to using archaic terms:

- Coloreds
- Morons
- Spastics
- Illegitimate children
- Mongoloids

Point out that the simplest solution to this problem is to remember that every individual is a *person* first, and to make a conscious effort to refer to people as people. Suggest that if labels cannot be avoided, they should be used as descriptive parts of speech, not as subjects (nouns). For example:

- "Roger is African American."
- "Grace is a person who is homeless."
- "Cindy is a person with Cerebral Palsy."
- "Ruben has a learning disability."
- "Lucy receives welfare."

Ask the students to consider the fact that they label others every day. Give a graphic example by moving past the group in a way that would be considered pretty ordinary except for the repetition of some small quirk, tick, or unusual move. Then ask the group: *How might you or other students label me? How would you refer to me in your conversations?*

Have the students form small groups of four to six. Ask them to take a couple of minutes to think about how others see them and to come up with a short label (one to three words) for themselves based on *how they think others see them.* Have the students take turns introducing themselves to the group using their first name and the label. (Examples: "Hi, I'm Aloof and Distant Denise" or "My name is Alex the Android.")

Next, direct the students to turn to the person on their right and observe that person silently for a moment or two. Have them think of a one-word label for the person based on their observations. Ask the students to combine the label with the person's first name and share it with the group. Examples might be, "Fat Frank" or "Queen Donna."

Finally, have the students pair up within their groups. Direct the partners to interview each other for 4 minutes (2 minutes each) before coming up with a one to three-word label for their partner based on what they reamed in the interview. Direct the students to introduce their partner to the group using the partner's first name plus the label.

In a follow-up discussion, ask the students to share with the entire group their feelings about the labels they gave and received.

Discussion questions:

1. How did you feel when you labeled yourself?
2. How did you feel when you were labeled by someone else?
3. How did you feel when you labeled someone else?
4. How often do we label others and why do we do it?
5. What effect does labeling have on our self-esteem? ...on our ability to really know one another? ...on our efforts to include all kinds of people?
6. What can we do to become more aware of our tendency to label others? How can we reverse that tendency?

I Wanted to Be Part of a Group, But Was Left Out
A Circle Session

Objectives:

The students will:

—understand and express the need to belong.

—describe an incident in which they were excluded.

—explain how the need to belong can influence individual behavior.

Introduce the Topic:

One of the most important things to most young people is fitting in—belonging to a group. Although this need continues into adulthood, it is particularly strong among young people, because this is the time when the skills of group membership are reamed. It is one of the main "developmental tasks" of youth. Today, we're going to look at what happens when we are refused membership in a group for some reason. We're going to talk about the feelings we experience when we are excluded. Our topic is, "I Wanted to Be Part of a Group, But Was Left Out"

Think back to a time when you really wanted to do something with a group of friends or an organization, but you weren't invited. How did you feel? What did you do? Maybe you tried out for a part in a play or a musical group and didn't make it How long did it take you to get over it? Have you ever heard some friends talking about something fun they did over the weekend and felt hurt because you weren't asked to join them? Have you ever tried to join in a conversation and been completely ignored? Have you ever felt that you were excluded because you were poorer than the other members of the group, or of a different race, or had a disability? Think about it for a few moments. If you decide to share, describe the situation and tell us how you handled your feelings. Our topic is, "I Wanted to Be Part of a Group, But Was Left Out."

Discussion questions:

1. What did you feel like doing when you were left out? What *did you* do?
2. How long did it take you to get over your hurt feelings?
3. If a group rejects you because you refuse to conform to its code of behavior, what's the best thing to do?
4. What advice would you give a friend who seemed willing to do almost anything to fit in with a group?
5. How do attitudes of exclusion hurt us?
6. What can you do to develop an attitude of inclusion?

How I Deal with Intolerance and Prejudice
A Circle Session

Objectives:
Group members will:
—describe their reactions to acts of intolerance and prejudice.
—evaluate the effectiveness of different kinds of responses.

Introduce the Topic:
Our topic today is, "How I Deal with Intolerance and Prejudice." Perhaps you can think of several different ways in which you have reacted to these things. If so, just tell us about the way you respond most often. You can describe your reaction to intolerance and prejudice directed at you, or directed at someone else in your presence. Or you might decide to tell us about intolerance and prejudice that you've discovered within yourself, and how you deal with that.

Do you get angry and challenge the other person? Do you show your disapproval with an icy stare and a cold manner? Are you assertive in expressing your opposing views? Or do you tend to ignore the person and act as if nothing happened? If you like, tell us about a specific time you responded this way, and describe how you felt. Our topic is, "How I Deal with Intolerance and Prejudice."

Discussion questions:
1. How well does your method of dealing with prejudice and intolerance work?
2. What happens as a result of your method? Are you satisfied with the results?
3. What would happen if all the people who usually ignore intolerance started opposing it assertively?

Additional Circle Session Topics
A Time When I Accepted Someone Else's Feelings
Someone Didn't Say a Word, But I Knew How S/he Felt
A Time I Showed Someone That I Cared
A Time I Felt Sorry for Someone Who Was Put Down
I Helped Someone Who Needed and Wanted My Help
A Time I Listened Well to Someone
Someone Who Always Understands Me
A Person I Can Share My Feelings With
How I Show Someone That I Understand
A Time I Could Have Shown That I Cared, But Didn't
A Time I Failed to Listen to Someone
A Time Someone Really Listened to Me
A Time Someone Failed to Listen to Me
One of the Most Caring People I Know
A Time Someone Understood My Point of View
A Time My Point of View Was Misunderstood

Communication

Activities in this unit teach students to:

- listen carefully and interpret information accurately.

- demonstrate the skills of attentive listening.

- recognize that communicating involves much more than the simple transmission of words and ideas.

Circle Sessions in this unit allow students to:

- describe the importance of listening in the communication process.

- identify effective listening behaviors.

Language As Pilot
A Communications Experiment

Objectives:
The students will:
—practice communicating clearly and accurately.
—describe problems caused by imprecise communication and differing interpretations.
—describe how they manage their behavior to achieve success when sightless.

Materials:
desks, tables, crumpled paper, and other objects generally available in the classroom

Procedure:
Begin by telling the students that you would like them to cooperate in conducting an experiment that relates to language and communication. Without any further explanation, ask the students to help you build a runway. Construct the runway out of furniture and people. Make it about 15 to 20 feet long and wide enough for a person to walk down. Next, litter the runway with debris, books, papers, pencils, and other small objects which will not cause a blindfolded person to trip or fall.

When the runway is ready, ask a student volunteer to role play the pilot of an airplane landing on the runway. Then ask a volunteer to play the part of the air-traffic controller trying to help the pilot land the plane by giving directions over an imaginary radio transmitter. As soon as two students volunteer, ask them to move to opposite ends of the runway.

Blindfold the pilot. Explain that a storm has hit and lightning has knocked out the transmitter of the plane. The receiver is still working so the pilot can get messages, but can't send them. Indicate that the storm has created havoc on the runway. Debris is all over the place. The control tower must try to land the plane without damage by sending directions over the radio. The visibility is zero, so the pilot must rely only on these messages for a safe landing. If the pilot brushes against any of the objects on the runway, the plane is considered crashed.

Allow several teams of pilots and controllers to attempt to land the plane safely. After each attempt, briefly discuss the problems each team encountered. Then ask the students to put the classroom back in order and return to their seats for a general discussion.

Discussion questions:
1. How did you feel when you were the pilot?
2. How did you compensate for being sightless?
3. How did you feel when you were the controller?
4. What specifically did you do to become your pilot's "eyes?"
5. How can we communicate clear and exact messages?
6. Has anything like this ever happened to you? Tell us about a time when you had trouble getting a precise message across or correctly understanding someone else's message.
7. What have you learned about language and communication from this experiment?
8. What did this experience teach you about functioning effectively with a disability? ...about working cooperatively with someone who has a disability?

Play It Back!
Dyad Sequence and Discussion

Objectives:

The students will:

—demonstrate attentive listening with a series of partners.

—explain how they let others know they are listening.

Materials:

chalkboard and chalk

Procedure:

Assign the students to groups of eight or ten. (An even number in each group is essential for this activity to work. If a group is one short, join that group during the activity.)

Ask the students to choose a partner. Explain that both people will take turns speaking to the same topic. As the first person (**A**) speaks for 1 minute, the second person (**B**) must listen very carefully, gathering information very much like a tape recorder. The listener should not interrupt or ask questions, except for clarification. When time is called, **B** will have 1 minute to "play back" to **A** as accurately as possible what he or she heard. Then **A** and **B** will switch roles. **B** will become the speaker and talk about the same topic for 1 minute while **A** listens. Then **A** will have 1 minute to "play back" what she or he heard. This will complete the first round, and the students will find new partners within their group.

Signal the end of each minute and give clear instructions. Conduct enough rounds so that every person is paired once with every other person in his or her group. (For example, if groups contain eight students, conduct seven rounds.)

Suggested Topics:

"My Favorite Hobby or Pastime"

"My Favorite Food"

"My Favorite TV Show or Movie"

"My Favorite Story, Poem, Book, or Magazine"

"My Favorite Animal"

"My Favorite Game or Sport"

"My Favorite Song or Musical Group"

"Something That Makes Me Happy"

"Something I Want To Do This Weekend"

"Something I'm Looking Forward To"

Discussion questions:

1. How did you feel as the speaker during this exercise?
2. How did you feel as the listener?
3. What was hardest about listening like a tape recorder?
4. Did speaking and/or listening get harder or easier as you went from partner to partner?
5. How does silent, attentive listening lead to effective communication? Why is it a good idea to "play back" what you hear?
6. What are some things you can do to show someone that you are really listening?
7. How can you let someone know that you are listening if he or she has a vision loss? ...a hearing loss?

Words Are Only Part of It
Dramatization and Discussion

Objectives:

The students will
—demonstrate that communication involves much more than the simple transmission of words and ideas.
—discuss how feelings are conveyed in communication.

Materials:

one copy of the experience sheet, "Body Talk," for each student;chalkboard and chalk

Procedure:

Prior to class, write the following words on the board:

delight	confusion
surprise	worry
hate	sadness
love	irritation
anger	fear

Begin the activity by briefly reviewing the list of words with the students. Explain that these are just some of the many emotions people feel. Point out that communication involves much more than the simple use of words. Emotions get into the act in a number of ways.

Illustrate the point by silently selecting one of the emotions listed on the board and asking the class to guess which one it is while you repeat a tongue twister. Say the tongue twister and, with your tone, inflection, facial expression, posture, and movements, simultaneously convey the emotion you selected. After the laughter subsides, allow the students to guess which emotion you were trying to convey. Then ask them how they knew. List the clues they mention on the board.

Repeat the tongue twister once or twice, conveying other emotions from the list. Discuss with the class the specific tones, inflection, facial expressions, body postures, and movements you used to express each feeling.

Invite the students to demonstrate other emotions. Have volunteers come to the front of the class and repeat the process. Introduce a new tongue twister from time to time. After each demonstration, ask the class to examine the manner in which the emotion was communicated. Ask questions such as:

1. Can you describe the tone and inflection?
2. What did his face do?
3. What was her posture like?
4. How did she move her body?

Tongue Twisters

- Rubber baby-buggy bumpers
- She sells sea shells by the sea shore.
- Peter Piper picked a peck of pickled peppers.
- How much wood would a woodchuck chuck if a woodchuck could chuck wood?
- Big black bugs bleed blood.

After some or all of the emotions listed have been demonstrated, vary the activity. Restrict what the performers can do. First, ask them not to move their bodies in any way, using words, tone, and inflection only. Second, ask them to convey the emotion completely nonverbally, depending only on facial expressions, posture, and body language.

Distribute the "Body Talk" experience sheet. Give the students a few minutes to fill it out. Lead a follow-up discussion.

Discussion Questions:

1. How do people communicate without words?
2. Why do you think tongue twisters were used in our dramatizations, instead of important ideas?
3. How can you hide your feelings when you are communicating with someone? What effect does that have on communication?
4. What did you learn from this activity? ...from the experience sheet?

Body Talk
Experience Sheet

You communicate with your body all the time. As you react emotionally to events in your life, your body takes on different postures and positions.

Think of a time recently when you experienced the following emotions. What did you do with your body? How do you think your body looked to others? Describe your body language below:

Embarrassment:

_____

_____

_____

_____

Nervousness:

_____

_____

_____

_____

Excitement:

_____

_____

_____

_____

Boredom:

_____

_____

_____

_____

Once When Somebody Wouldn't Listen To Me
A Circle Session

Objectives:
The students will:
—describe the importance of listening in the communication process.
—make verbal distinctions between attentive, conscious listening and inattentive, unconscious hearing.
—describe the need of people for attention and the consequences of not receiving it.

Introduce the Topic:
Say to the students: *Today we're going to talk about a common frustration that occurs in the communication process. Our topic is "Once When Someone Wouldn't Listen to Me."*

Did you ever need to have someone listen to you who wouldn't? Maybe the person you were talking to didn't agree with what you were saying and refused to listen. Or perhaps he or she was busy and didn't want to be bothered. How did you feel? You've probably noticed your little brother or sister, or seen a pet, like your dog or cat, trying to get someone's attention. People and animals can feel lost when they don't get needed attention, and it's especially important for people to be listened to when they need to talk about something. Take a minute to thing about it, and tell us about a time when you had an experience like this. The topic is "Once When Someone Wouldn't Listen to Me."

Discussion questions:
1. What similarities and differences did you notice in our feelings about not being listened to?
2. What can you do when you're not being listened to?
3. Should a person expect to be listened to every time he or she has something to say? Why or why not?
4. How did you feel when you are being ignored?

A Time I Listened Well
A Circle Session

Objectives:
The students will:
—describe a time when they listened effectively.
—identify effective listening behaviors.

Introduce the Topic:
Most of us appreciate having someone really listen to us. In this session we are going to turn this idea around and talk about how it feels to listen to someone else. The topic is, "A Time I Listened Well."

Can you remember a time when you really paid attention to someone and listened carefully to what he or she said. This means that you didn't interrupt with your own ideas or daydream about your own plans, but really concentrated and tried to understand what the other person was attempting to get across. Maybe you've listened to a friend like that, or a younger brother or sister, or a teacher or coach. Think about it for a few moments and, if you wish, tell us about, "A Time I Listened Well."

Discussion questions:
1. What kinds of things make listening difficult?
2. Why is it important to listen to others?
3. What could you do to improve your listening?
4. How do you feel when someone really listens to you?

Additional Circle Session Topics
A Time When Listening Would Have Kept Me Out of Trouble
I Told Someone How I Was Feeling
Something I See Differently Than My Parents See It
How I Used Sharing Circle Skills Outside the Circle
A Time I Said One Thing But Meant Another
A Time When I Communicated Well
What I Do to Make Myself Understood
A Time When Poor Communication Caused a Misunderstanding
What I Think Poor Communication Is
What I Think Good Communication Is

Group Dynamics

Activities in this unit teach students to:

- work cooperatively in teams to solve problems.

- identify specific differences that have contributed to a successful group endeavor.

- compare the feelings, performance, and commitment levels experienced when performing a task alone and in small groups.

Circles Sessions in this unit allow students to:

- discuss factors that cause people to associate (or not associate) in groups.

- develop an understanding of group dynamics and what it takes to get along with others.

Stepping Stones
Group Task and Discussion

Objectives:

The students will:

—work cooperatively in teams to solve a problem.

—identify effective and ineffective team behaviors.

Materials:

nine baseball bases (or any suitable substitute, such as cardboard squares or flattened paper bags) and an area (lawn, gym, or multipurpose room) at least 37 1/2 feet long.

Procedure:

Measure off 37 1/2 feet and mark both ends of the space. Group the class into teams of no more than ten and no fewer than seven each. (For example, 31 students could be divided into three groups of eight and one group of seven.) Allow *one less* stepping stone than there are team members. Subtract 2 1/2 feet from the length of the space for every team member *less than ten*, as follows:

    9 members = 35 feet
    8 members = 32 1/2 feet
    7 members = 30 feet

Explain to the students that you would like them to imagine that between the two markers there is a raging river. Their task is to get each team member across the river, using the bases as stepping stones. As each team attempts to cross the river, members must decide how to use their stepping stones to best advantage. This task involves trial, error, and team cooperation. Team members will need to experiment and help one another.

While the first team attempts to cross the river, the other teams should go to another room so that they cannot watch. This will allow each team to approach the problem without having seen another team work on it. On the other hand, do allow teams that have completed the task to watch the next teams attempt it. Laughter and encouragement on the part of observers will make the activity fun and interesting, but do not allow students to make derogatory statements or sounds.

Discussion questions:

1. What was the toughest part of this exercise for you? ...the most enjoyable part?
2. How did you work together? Did a leader emerge? How were problems resolved?
3. What did your team do that proved particularly effective? ...ineffective?
4. What did you see another team do that seemed particularly effective? ...ineffective?
5. What did you learn about teamwork from this activity?

Search for the One-Person Team
Group Discussion and Experience Sheet

Objectives:
The students will:
—state that successful teams are characterized by diversity.
—identify specific differences that have contributed to a successful group endeavor.
—distinguish between individual and group identity.
—distinguish between interdependence and dependence.

Materials:
one copy of the experience sheet "Search for the One-Person Team" for each student

Procedure:
Introduce the experience sheet by making the point that rarely is a successful endeavor accomplished by one person acting alone. Even when a single individual appears to have masterminded and carried out a project single-handedly, there are always other people in the background without whose cooperation and collaboration the finished product would not have been achieved.

Announce to the students that you want each of them to identify a group that is diverse and interdependent, and identify the different skills and talents that make the group successful. Explain that the students may choose any type of group they wish: a band, singing group, athletic team, club, business, etc. The group may be one to which they belong, or it may be a group they have observed in action or read about. A solo performer who works with a backup team or a support crew may also be considered a group.

Have the students turn to the experience sheet, "Search for the One-Person Team," and announce that they will have about 15 minutes to complete the sheet.

When the students have completed their experience sheets, ask volunteers to tell the class about the diverse make-up of the group they selected. After those students who wish to have shared, make the following points:

- No one can succeed in complete isolation.
- We all have gifts to contribute and those gifts are needed somewhere.
- Generally speaking, teams accomplish more than individuals accomplish.
- When we choose to be *interdependent* with others, we are not becoming a *dependent* person, we are joining our resources with the resources of others in a common effort.

Conclude the activity by facilitating further discussion.

Discussion questions:

1. What is the difference between interdependence and dependence?
2. How does diversity make a group successful?
3. When you think about the group or team you selected, do you judge the group by thinking about individual members or by thinking about the group as a whole? Why do you think that is?
4. Can you think of a person who succeeded at something without interdepending with others?

Search for the One-Person Team
Experience Sheet

When people come together, they bring all of their unique personalities, viewpoints, talents, and skills. When they use these differences to work toward a common goal, wonderful things often happen. Take a moment to think of some groups and teams that you know about. Pick a group or team that you think is successful because each member brings something special and important to the process. Then answer the following questions:

What is the name of the group? _____

What does the group do? _____

What talents or skills do members of the group have?

_____

_____

Can you name all the members of this group? Name and describe as many as you can:

	Name	Description
1.	_____	_____
2.	_____	_____
3.	_____	_____
4.	_____	_____
5.	_____	_____

What makes this group stand out? _____

_____

Alphabet Names
Testing Team Synergy

Objectives:

The students will:

—compare the feelings, performance, and commitment levels experienced when performing a task alone and in small groups.

—describe how individual motivation affects individual performance.

—describe how individual and group motivation affects group synergy.

Materials:

individual writing materials, and one sheet of chart paper and magic marker for each small group

Procedure:

Have each student take out a sheet of paper. Instruct the students to list the letters of the alphabet from "A" through "Z" in a vertical column down the left side of the sheet.

Randomly select a sentence from any document and read aloud the first twenty-six letters in that sentence. Tell the students to write these letters in a second vertical column to the right of the first. Every student should end up with the same twenty-six sets of letters.

Tell the students that they now have 10 minutes to individually record the names of famous people whose initials correspond with the twenty-six sets of letters. The people can be politicians, authors, inventors, film stars, musicians, etc. Only one name may be recorded for each set of initials. Announce that the maximum score is twenty-six points, one for each legitimate name.

At the end of 10 minutes, have the students exchange and "grade" each other's papers. Allow a few moments to verify any questionable names. Then have the students call out their scores while you jot them on the board. Circle the high score and ask the students to see who can be the first to compute and call out the average score. Write the average on the board, too.

Have the students form teams of five to eight. Give each team a sheet of chart paper and a magic marker. Have each team choose a recorder. Announce that, working together as a team, the students have 10 minutes to develop a second list of famous names. Have the recorder list the letters of the alphabet in a vertical column on the chart paper; then read the first 26 letters from a newly selected passage of text.

Call time after 10 minutes and check the lists. Record the team scores and average score on the board. Compare them with the individual scores. Then lead a discussion, focusing on the differences in motivation, frustration, enjoyment, and achievement experienced working individually and in teams.

Discussion questions:

1. How did your individual score compare with your team score?
2. What feelings did you have working individually? ...working with a team?
3. How well did your team work together?
4. Which did you experience most when working individually, a sense of competition or collaboration? Why?
5. Which (competition or collaboration) did you experience most when working with a team? Why?
6. Were you more motivated to think of names when you were working alone or as part of a team? Why?
7. What did you learn from this activity?

A Group I Like Belonging To
A Circle Session

Objectives:
Group members will:
—describe the benefits of belonging to specific groups.
—discuss factors that cause people to associate (or not associate) in groups.

Introduce the Topic:
Today our topic is, "A Group I Like Belonging To." One of the most important things in life for most of us is being part of a group of people whom we enjoy and with whom we share common interests or goals. So today we're going to talk about groups we belong to and how it feels to be part of those groups.

If you decide to share, tell us about one group that you consider yourself a part of. The group can be a club or organization here at school, or one that exists outside of school. It can also be a group of friends — students who like each other and hang around together. After you tell us about the group, describe one thing the group does that you enjoy, how you contribute to the group, what the group contributes to you, and how you feel about belonging. Today's topic is, "A Group I Like Belonging To."

Discussion questions:
1. Why do people join groups, clubs, and organizations?
2. What drew you into the group you described?
3. Why are some people "loners" who rarely associate with groups?
4. How can a group give the impression that it is open to new members?

Something I Like to Do With Other People
A Circle Session

Objective:

To help students to develop an understanding of group dynamics, what it takes to get along with others, and to enhance self-awareness by discussing what brings them pleasure.

Introduce the Topic:

In your own words, say to the students: *Today's topic is, "Something I Like to Do With Other People." It's fun to do things with other people. Most games require two or more people, as do many sports, such as football, baseball, even tennis. Think of something you like to do with other people. It might be shopping or talking on the phone. Perhaps you like big family picnics or holiday dinners. Or maybe you enjoy having lunch with friends. Do you have more fun at amusement parks when you are with a group? Think of one thing you like to do with other people and tell us about it. The topic is, "Something I Like to Do With Other People."*

Discussion questions:

1. What do we gain by experiencing events and activities with other people?
2. What happens when a group gets too large for a particular activity? What are the effects of having too few people?
3. What are some things you do when you're with others to show you're a good group member?

Additional Circle Session Topics

We Cooperated to Get It Done
A Skill or Talent I Brought to the Team
A Time I Let the Team Down
A Role I Play in Groups
My Favorite Team
Something I Did That Helped the Team Succeed
A Way I Show Respect for Others
We Compromised to Get It Done
When the Easy Way Out Made Things Worse
A Time I Didn't Want to Be a Member of a Group
A Time I Felt Included
I Went Out of My Way to Include Someone Else
What I Think Makes a Winning Team
I Contributed Something Important to the Group
A Time I Felt Left Out
A Time I Worked in a Successful Group

Conflict Resolution

Activities in this unit teach students to:

- Assess the effectiveness of their typical behaviors when angry.

- develop rules to ensure that conflicts are handled fairly.

- describe how different perceptions can lead to conflict.

Circle Sessions in this unit allow students to:

- examine and discuss real conflicts they have experienced.

- describe positive ways of responding to put-downs.

Assessing Anger Styles
Discussion and Experience Sheet

Objectives:

The students will:

—identify two recent events that caused them to feel angry and describe what they did in each situation.

—Assess the effectiveness of their typical behaviors when angry.

—Examine and discuss several common "anger styles."

—Explain how they can choose more effective responses in situations that provoke anger.

Materials:

one copy of the experience sheet, "Assessing Your anger" for each student; chalkboard

Information to Share:

Anger is a normal emotion. We all have characteristic ways of expressing anger. For purposes of this activity, these are called *anger styles*. Although anger styles are probably learned (as opposed to inborn), they are deeply engrained and therefore automatic—almost like reflexes. The results our anger styles produce have reinforced our tendency to repeat them over the years. Still, they may not be the most effective or productive behaviors to use in every situation. Learning to consciously choose how we express our anger will help us become better managers of conflict.

Procedure:

Write the word *anger* on the board. Ask the students what kind of feelings the word or subject causes them to experience. Listen to their responses, jotting notes on the board.

Explain that the class is going to discuss the subject of anger in some depth, but first you want the students to help by individually answering some questions.

Distribute the experience sheet, "Assessing Anger," and quickly go over the directions. Give the students 10 minutes to fill out the sheet. Encourage quiet reflection.

Call time. Have the students choose partners and briefly share what they have written.

Convene the entire group and ask volunteers to tell the class what "style" they typically use to express their anger. Write their contributions on the board, generating a list of anger styles. Fill in with suggestions of your own until your list covers all of the styles listed below (it may include more). Once a style is listed, acknowledge additional examples of that style by putting a check mark after the descriptor.

Anger Styles

- Blowing up/attacking
- Withdrawing, refusing to talk
- Suppressing, denying, hiding feelings
  —pretending, being phoney
  —use of alcohol and/or other drugs
  —overeating
  —excessive TV
- Getting even
  —in hidden ways (passive-aggressive)
  —openly, through punishment
- Displacing feelings (taking them out on someone/something else)
- Releasing anger through stress-reduction
  —exercise
  —tasks/chores that require physical activity
  —relaxation/music/meditation
  —talking with a friend, parent, counselor, etc.
- Assertively confronting the situation
  —explaining the problem and your feelings
  —attacking the problem, *not* the person.

Conclude the activity with a discussion about how anger styles are developed and what purposes they serve (see "Information to Share"). Stress the need to decide when a style is productive and when it is not, and to consciously choose to respond in alternative ways when a style is not effective.

Discussion questions:

1. How do we develop our styles of expressing anger?
2. Why do we persist in behaving in ways that don't work?
3. Why is anger such a difficult emotion to deal with?
4. Under what circumstances would it be best to use stress-reduction techniques to deal with your anger, rather than confront the other person?
5. What skills do you need to have in order to assertively confront a situation or person and try to solve the problem that caused your anger?

Extension:

Have the students do cost-benefit analyses of the major anger styles. Form groups of about six students, and assign each group a different style. Distribute chart paper and markers. Have a recorder in each group write the anger style as a heading across the top of a sheet. In two vertical columns, one labeled *Benefits* (+), the other labeled *Costs* (-), have the students brainstorm and list positive and negative outcomes, fallout, feelings, etc., that can occur as a result of using that style. Have the groups share their lists with the class. Discuss.

Assessing Your Anger
Experience Sheet

Try to remember two recent incidents in which you became angry. Taking one incident at a time, think carefully about what happened and answer these questions as honestly as you can.

Anger Incident #1

What caused your anger?

How intense were your feelings?

Mildly Annoyed ———————————|———————————— **Furious**

How did your body feel?

What were your thoughts?

What did you feel like doing?

What *did* you do?

What was the result?

How effective was your behavior? Did it make matters a lot worse, or did it produce the results you wanted without hurting anyone? Explain:

Anger Incident #2

What caused your anger?

How intense were your feelings?

Mildly Annoyed |————————————————————| **Furious**

How did your body feel?

What were your thoughts?

What did you feel like doing?

What *did* you do?

What was the result?

How effective was your behavior? Did it make matters a lot worse, or did it produce the results you wanted without hurting anyone? Explain:

Rules for a Fair Fight
Imagery, Discussion, and Small-Group Brainstorming

Objectives:
The students will:
—describe the similarities between a conflict and a game or sport.
—develop rules intended to ensure that conflicts are handled fairly.

Materials:
chart paper and markers for each work group; masking tape; chalkboard

Information to Share:
Conflict is normal. While most of us don't go out the door each morning looking for conflicts, we tend to encounter one or two just about every day. If we think of conflict as a contest—like a tennis match or a game of volleyball—we recognize that it is a *cooperative event*, a challenge, a test of skills. If we really want to perform well on the conflict court, we have to know the rules of the sport, avoid making too many fouls, present ourselves and our ideas in the most effective ways possible, and respect the rights of our opponent. We have to fight fair. Guidelines for fighting fair might include:

- Identify and focus on the problem.
- Attack the problem, not the person.
- Listen to your opponent.
- Demonstrate respect.
- Take responsibility for your own actions.

Procedure:
Ask the students to think of a sport or game they enjoy playing—baseball, chess, tennis, volleyball, wrestling, basketball, Monopoly, Scrabble, etc. Tell them to take a few moments, close their eyes, and imagine themselves playing that game with a skilled opponent, being totally involved and energized.

Now, without opening their eyes, ask the students to recall a recent conflict they had with another person—anything from a mild disagreement to a noisy fight. Tell them to picture this contest in as much detail as possible.

Next, suggest that the students allow their minds to transform that image of conflict into a sport or game, seeing it as a contest of opposing ideas, opinions, beliefs, perceptions—whatever it actually was. The opponents in the conflict may not agree, but the fact that they are interacting means that they are playing this game *cooperatively*.

Invite the students to open their eyes and comment on this imagery experience. Generate a discussion about the analogy of conflict as game or sport. Encourage the students to further develop the notion, while making key points of your own (see "Information to Share").

On the chalkboard, write this heading:

RULES FOR A FAIR FIGHT

Ask the students to form work groups of five to eight, and choose a recorder. Distribute the chart paper and markers.

Tell the groups that you want them to brainstorm a list of rules for the game of conflict. In your own words say to them: *Your list doesn't have to be long, but it should accomplish certain things. Rules ensure an even start, safety, and adherence to certain agreed-upon behaviors throughout the game. Rules protect both the players and the object of the game. It may help to think about the rules of a specific sport or game and keep those in mind as you work.*

Allow 10-15 minutes for brainstorming. Then have the groups display their lists and share them with the class. Facilitate a culminating discussion.

Discussion questions:

1. What are some of the benefits of thinking of conflict as a game with rules?
2. When you are in a conflict, how can you encourage the other person to "fight fair."
3. What can you say or do when the other person keeps breaking the rules?
4. What have you learned about conflict from this exercise?

Extension:

If time permits, have the groups brainstorm a second list—a list of GAME FOULS. Explain that, just as in a sport, fouls are behaviors that are not allowed because they create an unfair advantage, are disrespectful or dangerous, or destroy the object of the game. Have the groups display and explain their two lists, side-by-side.

Everyone's Got a Point of View
Creative Writing, Discussion, and Sharing

Objectives:

The students will:

—describe different perceptions of the same situation.

—describe how different perceptions can lead to conflict.

Materials:

the story, "The Maligned Wolf," and writing materials

Procedure:

Begin by defining the word *maligned*: (Maligned means abused, ill-treated, slandered, assailed, etc.) Then read the story "The Maligned Wolf."

Discussion questions:

After you've read the story, facilitate a discussion with the class by asking such questions as:

1. Can you remember how you felt about the wolf as a child, when you heard the story, "Little Red Riding Hood?"
2. How do you feel about the wolf now?
3. How have your feelings changed about the Grandmother, the Lumberjack, and Little Red Riding Hood?
4. Can you think of times in your own life when you had very definite feelings about a situation until you heard another side to the story? Who would like to give an example?
5. What was the purpose of this story?

Explain the writing assignment. Following the discussion, ask the students to pick a

character from another classic story and rewrite the story from the villain's point of view. Suggested villains/stories are:

> The Giant in "Jack and the Beanstalk"
> The Queen in "Snow White"
> The Spider in "Little Miss Muffet"
> A Stepsister in "Cinderella"

Brainstorm additional stories, listing all ideas on the chalkboard. Then ask the students to begin writing. Have the students complete their stories at home, or allow time during a subsequent class period.

Note: Greater creativity and enjoyment may be generated by having the students write their stories in pairs or small groups.

Conclusion:

Have the students share their stories in small groups or with the total class. If the small-group method is used, remind the students to follow circle session rules and procedures.

Extension:

- Ask the students to convert their stories into short dramas. Conduct a class reaction session following each enactment.
- Ask the students to write about one of the following topics:
  "When Someone Understood My Point of View"
  "When Someone Misunderstand My Point of View"
  "At First I Didn't Understand Someone's Point of View"

The Maligned Wolf
A Short Story

By Lief Fearn

The forest was my home. I lived there and I cared about it. I tried to keep it neat and clean. Then one sunny day, while I was cleaning up some garbage a camper had left behind, I heard footsteps. I leaped behind a tree and saw a rather plain little girl coming down the trail carrying a basket. I was suspicious of this little girl right away because she was dressed funny—all in red, and her head covered up so it seemed like she didn't want people to know who she was. Naturally, I stopped to check her out. I asked who she was, where she was going, where she had come from, and all that. She gave me a song and dance about going to her grandmother's house with a basket of lunch. She appeared to be a basically honest person, but she was in my forest and she certainly looked suspicious with that strange getup of hers. So I decided to teach her just how serious it is to prance through the forest unannounced and dressed funny.

I let her go on her way, but I ran ahead to her grandmother's house. When I saw that nice old woman, I explained my problem and she agreed that her granddaughter needed to learn a lesson, all right. The old woman agreed to stay out of sight until I called her.
Actually, she hid under the bed.

When the girl arrived, I invited her into the bedroom where I was in the bed, dressed like the grandmother. The girl came in all rosy-cheeked and said something nasty about my big ears. I've been insulted before so I made the best of it by suggesting that my big ears would help me to hear better. Now, what I meant was that I liked her and wanted to pay close attention to what she was saying. But she makes another insulting crack about my bulging eyes. Now you can see how I was beginning to feel about this girl who put on such a nice front, but was apparently a very nasty person. Still, I've made it a policy to turn the other cheek, so I told her that my big eyes helped me to see her better.

Her next insult really got to me. I've got this problem with having big teeth. And that little girl made an insulting crack about them. I know that I should have had better control, but I leaped up from that bed and growled that my teeth would help me to eat her better.

Now let's face it—no wolf could ever eat a little girl—everyone knows that—but that crazy girl started running around the house screaming—me chasing her to calm her down. I'd taken off the grandmother clothes, but that only seemed to make it worse. And all of a sudden the door came crashing open and a big lumberjack is standing there with his axe. I looked at him and all of a sudden it became clear that I was in trouble. There was an open window behind me and out I went.

I'd like to say that was the end of it. But that Grandmother character never did tell my side of the story. Before long the word got around that I was a mean, nasty guy. Everybody started avoiding me. I don't know about that little girl with the funny red outfit, but I didn't live happily ever after. In fact, now us wolves are practically extinct! And I'm sure that little girl's story has had a lot to do with it!

I Was Involved in a Misunderstanding
A Circle Session

Objectives:

The students will:

—identify missing information and faulty communication as two main causes of misunderstandings.

—describe ways of handling misunderstandings that can prevent their escalation.

Introduce the Topic:

Sometimes conflicts occur because one or both people don't have enough information about each other's ideas, feelings, or actions. They simply don't understand each other. Let's talk about times like these today. Our topic is, "I Was Involved in a Misunderstanding."

Tell us about a time when some piece of information was missing and it caused either you or another person to draw the wrong conclusion. Maybe you didn't understand a friend's reason for making a particular decision, or maybe the friend didn't understand yours. Perhaps you said something that the other person took the wrong way because it was out of context. Or it could have been a situation in which you or the other person misunderstood instructions and ended up doing the wrong thing. Misunderstandings don't have to lead to conflict, but they sometimes do. Tell us how you handled yours. The topic is, "I Was Involved in a Misunderstanding."

Discussion questions:

1. What strategies for handling misunderstandings seemed to work particularly well in the situations we shared?

2. Since misunderstandings are usually unintentional, what are some things we can do to make sure they don't escalate into conflict?

3. How does good communication figure in the prevention of misunderstandings? ...in their resolution?

A Time Someone Put Me Down, But I Handled It Well
A Circle Session

Objectives:

The students will:

—describe positive ways of responding to put-downs.

—explain how put-downs can lead to conflict and violence.

Introduce the Topic:

Our topic today involves some of the language of conflict. It has to do with words — and the way they're spoken — that tend to cause hurt, resentment, and anger. But it also has to do with our ability to control ourselves and prevent conflict. The topic is, "A Time Someone Put Me Down, But I Handled It Well."

Think of a situation in which you felt someone really put you down. Maybe the person called you a name, or made a negative comment about your appearance or something you did. Perhaps you were trying to be friendly with someone and that person rudely rejected you. Maybe the put-down was done unknowingly or as a joke, or perhaps the person did it deliberately. In any case, you were able to withstand the remark and control your emotions and behavior. Tell us how you did that. What did you say to yourself in order to stay "up" when someone put you down. Please don't mention any names. The topic is, "A Time Someone Put Me Down, But I Handled It Well."

Discussion questions:

1. Why do people put each other down?
2. What effective ways of reacting to put downs did you hear in the circle today?
3. How can a simple put-down lead to violence?
4. What did you learn from this session about preventing conflict? ...about your own communication behaviors?

Additional Circle Session Topics

I Got Blamed for Something I Didn't Do
How Conflict Makes Me Feel
A Time When Sharing Prevented a Fight
How I Helped a Friend Resolve a Conflict
I Got Into a Fight Because I Was Already Feeling Upset
A Time I Was Afraid to Face a Conflict
Something That Really Bothers Me
I Observed a Conflict
I Accidentally Made Somebody Mad
I Started a Conflict Between My Friends
A Time Humor Saved the Day
We Resolved a Conflict By Ourselves
A Time I Listened Well to Someone I Disagreed With

Jalmar Press and Innerchoice Publishing are happy to announce

a collaborative effort under which all Innerchoice titles will now be distributed

only through Jalmar Press.

To request the latest catalog of our joint resources for use by teachers,

counselors and other care-givers to empower children to develop inner-

directed living and learning skills,

call us at: (800) 662-9662

or fax us at: (310) 816-3092

or send us a card to: P.O. Box 1185, Torrance, CA 90505

We're eager to serve you and the students you work with.

By the way, Jalmar Press / Innerchoice Publishing have a new series coming

up that can give you all the necessary tools to deal with the tough stuff that

you face on a daily basis.

The new "HELPING YOU DEAL WITH THE TOUGH STUFF" SERIES" is meant to be

your best friend as you do your job.

Ten titles will be available in the fall of 1999.
Write or call for the latest information or to place your order.

to be smart

The Original Warm Fuzzy Tale
by Claude Steiner
Pre-K - Adult

The classic original story about Warm Fuzzies and Cold Pricklies. A charming fairy tale. Adventure, fantasy, heroes, villains, and a moral: the more good you share, the more good you get.
A great resource.
A lovely gift book.
It reminds you of the important things in life.
JP9008, $9.95, 48pp.

<u>Cassette:</u> Songs of Warm Fuzzy
JP9003, $12.95

Squib, The Owl

Grades K-12, 64-80 pp, 8.5x11
Written and illustrated by Larry Shles

Moths and Mothers, Feathers and Fathers - The story of Squib, The Owl begins.
JP9057, $ 9.95

Hugs and Shrugs - Squib's reflection in the pond shows he's lost a piece of himself. He discovers it fell in, not out!
JP9047, $ 9.95

Do I Have to Go to School Today? Squib is afraid the school bus will swallow him.
JP9062, $ 9.95

Hoots & Toots & Hairy Brutes - Squib can only toot. He sets out to learn how to give a mighty hoot.
JP9056, $ 9.95

Aliens in my Nest - What does it feel like to face an older brother turned adolescent?
JP9049, $ 9.95

Scooter's Tail of Terror - Introduces a new forest character - a squirrel named Scooter in a fable of addiction and hope.
JP9089, $ 9.95

All six books: JP9049, $40.00

TA for Tots PreK-3
JP9073, $19.95,
144pp, 8.5x11
Coloring Book
JP9033, $1.95

I'm OK Poster $3
JP9002, $3.00

TA for Kids Grades 4-9
JP9009, 12.95,
112pp, 8.5x11

These books have helped thousands of young children and their parents to better understand and relate to each other. Helps youngsters understand their intrinsic worth as human beings. Builds and strengthens self-esteem, esteem of others, personal and social responsibility, critical thinking, and independent judgement. These books recognize that each person is a unique being with the capability to learn, grow and develop. Great for parents and other care-givers.

MEMO

No.	Book	Qty.
IP9032	50 Act./EQ Lvl I	
IP9033	50 Act/EQ Lvl II	
IP9037	50 Act/EQ Lvl III	
IP9038	Talking w/Kids	
BA7506	Em. Intell. Book	
NP4307	Em. Intell. Video	
IP9034	EQ/Counseling	
JP9008	Warm Fuzzy Tale	
JP9003	Warm Fuzzy Cass.	
JP9049	Squib, the Owl	
JP9073	TA for Tots	
JP9033	Coloring Book	
JP9002	I'm OK Poster	
JP9009	TA for Kids	

Order toll free 800/662-9662

Talking With Kids: Guided Discussions for Developing Emotional Intelligence

Guided discussions are the EQ super-strategy and this book is chock full of them! What better way to develop the emotional intelligence of your students than by participation in relevant discussions about things that are important to them. This powerful and versatile instructional strategy is unusually effective as a tool for developing —

- **self-awareness**
- **self-control**
- **the ability to understand and manage feelings**
- **empathy**
- **cooperation**
- **responsibility**
- **communication**
- **strategies for managing conflict and stress, and**
- **group interaction skills**

Included in this book:

- 89 fully developed guided discussion topics
- Suggestions for introducing each topic to students
- Key questions to ask to facilitate higher level thinking, discovery, and insight
- A comprehensive introduction to Emotional Intelligence
- Step-by-step instructions for leading Guided Discussions
- Suggestions for organizing Guided Discussions and managing the rest of the class
- Guidelines for developing your own Guided Discussion topics

INNERCHOICE PUBLISHING
P.O. BOX 1185 • TORRANCE, CA 90505
Tel. (310) 816-3085 Fax (310) 816-3092